SESSIONS WITH MARK

Smyth & Helwys Publishing, Inc.
6316 Peake Road
Macon, Georgia 31210-3960
1-800-747-3016
© 2008 by Smyth & Helwys Publishing
All rights reserved.
Printed in the United States of America.

The paper used in this publication meets the minimum
requirements of American National Standard for Information
Sciences—Permanence of Paper for Printed Library Materials.

Library of Congress Cataloging-in-Publication Data

*Sessions with Mark : following Jesus at full speed / by Michael
D. McCullar and Rickey Letson. p. cm. Includes bibliographical
references (p.). ISBN 978-1-57312-517-8 (pbk. : alk. paper)
1. Bible. N.T. Mark—Textbooks. I. Letson, Rickey. II. Title.
BS2585.55.M33 2008 226.3'07—dc22 2008048429*

Sessions *with*
••• Mark

Following Jesus *at Full Speed*

Michael D. McCullar & Rickey Letson

SMYTH&HELWYS
PUBLISHING INCORPORATED · MACON, GEORGIA

Dedications

To Lisa McCullar, an inspiration for loving
To the memory of Karla Hurst Davis, an inspiration for living
To the memory of Benjamin Blackburn, an inspiration for learning
—M. M.

To Ann Marie, Callie, and Caleb, I love you all.
—R. L.

Table of Contents

Introducing Mark vii

Session 1 1
All Cleaned Up and Somewhere to Go: Jesus' Baptism
Mark 1:1-11

Session 2 11
Back to Nature: The Parable of the Sower
Mark 4:1-20

Session 3 23
Jesus and the Demoniac
Mark 5:1-20

Session 4 35
Blind Familiarity: Jesus in His Hometown
Mark 6:1-6

Session 5 45
The Great Fish Sandwich Lesson
Mark 6:30-44

Session 6 57
Jesus on Divorce
Mark 10:1-9

Session 7 67
Jesus and the Rich Young Ruler
Mark 10:17-27

Session 8 77
Jesus on Fig Trees and Temples
Mark 11:11-18

Session 9 87
The Might of Mites: The Widow's Mite
Mark 12:38-44

Session 10 95
Excited and Unafraid: The Unexpected Conclusion
to the Gospel
Mark 16:1-20

Bibliography 105

Introducing Mark

In his book on Mark's Gospel, R. Alan Cole says, "The basic questions of Christianity are always the same: Who was Jesus? What is salvation? What is the good news? Why should we preach it?" (12). Mark, the second book of the New Testament, does an excellent job of answering these questions and providing foundation and framework to the life and times of Jesus Christ. Mark's account is one of the three Synoptic Gospels, along with Matthew and Luke. Each writer provides a synopsis of the life, teachings, and actions of Jesus. William Barclay explains, "The word *synoptic* comes from two Greek words which mean *to see together;* and these three are called Synoptic Gospels because they can be set down in parallel columns and their common matter looked at together" (*The Gospel of Mark,* 1). When John's work is added, the first four books of the New Testament become the letters of the "four evangelists."

It is now commonly believed that Mark was written before either Matthew or Luke, making it the earliest Synoptic Gospel. However, early church fathers held that Matthew was the initial Gospel writing because he was directly associated with Jesus and he wrote a patently Hebrew-focused Gospel account. Later scholarship disavowed the Matthew-first school of thought for several reasons, the primary one being that both Matthew and Luke appear to borrow liberally from Mark in structure and content. David Garland writes, "Matthew and Luke testify to Mark's authority since they allowed themselves to be guided by him when they wrote their own Gospels" (27). William Barclay wraps up this argument with his statistical assessments of the three synoptic accounts:

When we study the matter closely we find that Mark can be divided into 105 sections. Of these, ninety-three occur in Matthew and eighty-one in Luke. Only four are not included either in Matthew or in Luke. Even more compelling is this. Mark has 661 verses; Matthew has 1,068; Luke has 1,149 verses. Of Mark's 661 verses, Matthew reproduces no fewer than 606. Sometimes he alters the wording slightly but he even reproduces 51 percent of Mark's actual words. Of Mark's 661 verses, Luke reproduces 320, and he actually uses 53 percent of Mark's actual words. Of the fifty-five verses of Mark which Matthew does not reproduce, thirty-one are found in Luke. So the result is that there are only twenty-four verses in Mark which do not occur somewhere in Matthew or Luke. (*The Gospel of Mark*, 2)

A logical conclusion is that Mark's work was used as a guide by Matthew and Luke, making him (Mark) the first Gospel writer. It is important to note two things: First, while there are striking similarities in the three accounts, each author wrote to a different audience; and second, it is a good thing that plagiarism attorneys did not exist in the first-century Greco-Roman world!

Author and Date

The author of this letter does not identify himself, but scholarly consensus points to Peter's assistant, Mark. Is this the same John Mark who was an associate of Peter, Paul, and Barnabas (Acts 12:12; Col 4:10; 2 Tim 4:11)? Mark was one of the most common male names of that era, so it is impossible to know with certainty, and there are no firm alternatives for another knowledgeable and well-connected author named Mark. The early church fathers were virtually unified in the belief that Mark, the interpreter and chronicler of Peter, authored this account of Jesus. Darrell L. Bock quotes Clement:

> The Gospel according to Mark had this occasion. As Peter had preached the word publicly at Rome, and declared the Gospel by the Spirit, many who were present requested that Mark, who had followed him for a long time and remembered his sayings, should write them out. And having composed the Gospel he gave it to those who had requested it. (394)

Opinions vary greatly as to when Mark's Gospel was written, so determining a date for authorship has never been a cohesive process.

There are those who see Mark writing in Rome with Peter, while others view this account as a post-Peter effort. If Mark composed this letter while with Peter in Rome, it would be dated as early as mid-late 50s. On the other hand, if this account was written after Peter was killed, the date could have been as late as AD 70, the year Rome successfully fought back against the Jews in Jerusalem and destroyed the temple. The difference in years is both large and important to a thorough assessment of this Gospel.

In that span of approximately fifteen years, the world and religious order changed radically. Rome easily dispensed with the Hebrew uprising and changed the entire landscape of Jerusalem. Since Mark did not use the apocalyptic approach John used in his three epistles and in Revelation, it could be argued that the temple had not yet been destroyed.

It is also worth considering the dates of Nero's reign as caesar (AD 54–68). Had Mark been writing at the later date, he likely would have mentioned the atrocities Nero perpetuated against the Christians. When these factors are considered, it becomes anyone's guess as to when the letter was written. Fortunately, most modern readers of the Bible don't place a high priority on a definite date of authorship; the content and the contextual insights enable modern Christians who study Scripture to find Jesus in new and powerful ways.

Mark's Unique Writing Style

Mark's account was written through a lens of action; there are no lulls in his writing. It would be easy to believe that Mark would not have sat still long enough to record the Sermon on the Mount. He describes Jesus as a person of intense passion, energy, and drive. Mark records only four of Jesus' parables but includes eighteen miracles. As the *Life Application Bible Commentary* states, "He is interested in Christ's *works*, not just his *words*" (Barton et al., xi).

Mark skimps on words in general; his is the shortest Gospel account of Jesus. He skips the genealogy of Jesus and ancient prophecies, and he assumes that the unique birth sequence was not important enough to include. When we consider that Mark's audience was Roman, these characteristics are easier to understand. Matthew wrote almost exclusively to a Jewish audience, so profiling Jesus' *bona fide's* was of the utmost importance. Matthew *qualified* Jesus as the Messiah. Roman Gentiles had no conception of a messiah and would not have appreciated twenty pages of qualifying statements. Rome was about action—and action was what Mark delivered. Mark portrayed Jesus as powerful yet benevolent: healing the sick, calming storms, exorcising demons, raising the dead, restoring sight to the blind. Mark's Jesus was God on a mission.

Critics of his writing style have called Mark "clumsy." It is true that he is not the smoothest of the biblical writers, and it is also true that he takes some license with chronological events. Mark has been described as using the "sandwich" method in his listing of acts and events in the life of Jesus. His not-quite-chronological grouping system was used for effect and impact, but it never lessened the Gospel account in any way. An example of the "Markan sandwich" is the cursing of the fig tree and the temple cleansing episodes. Mark clearly "sandwiched" the temple cleansing between the two fig tree events. Alan Culpepper writes,

> The cursing of the fig tree is intercalated with the demonstration in the temple in Mark, creating a typical "Markan sandwich" in which the two events are to be considered together, each providing a context for interpreting the other. Matthew and Luke both smooth out the chronology. Luke omits the cursing of the fig tree altogether, while Matthew places it on the day after Jesus' prophetic action in the temple. By doing so, however, the effect of the cursing on the tree must be immediate, and its association with Jesus' action in the temple is diminished. (372)

Mark's "sandwich" approach gives a deeper understanding and relevance to the events surrounding Jesus. It is obvious that the chronology was not as important to Mark as was the message. When you consider that no one knows the exact sequence of events anyway, Mark becomes even more of a visionary.

Relevance for Today

If you asked a group of Christians, "What's your favorite Gospel account?" you would likely get votes for each of the first four writers. Sadly, however, at the tally's end, Mark would likely come in last. This would be especially true if the vote was taken in December, as Mark does not include the birth account. Mark also seems to lose points for brevity. Simply put, Mark's Gospel is a very short account of Jesus' life and ministry. While there's no such thing as a bad short sermon, some people do find fault in a short Synoptic Gospel. Mark also skips the majority of Jesus' teachings and thus has the least amount of "red" letters. If the number of red letters determines the validity of a biblical book, Mark loses. On the other hand, Mark excels in depicting an active Jesus who works powerful miracles in order to proclaim the coming of God's kingdom. It's a sure bet that Jesus drew bigger crowds for healings and exorcisms than he did for sermons and lessons. This is the Jesus of Mark's account.

In many ways, Mark is the most viable Gospel account for today's world. When life grows difficult and faith grows weak, it is the sovereign power of God in action that provides hope and certainty. The Jesus of Mark's Gospel account is both savior and hero.

All Cleaned Up and
Somewhere to Go:
Jesus' Baptism

Mark 1:1-11

Several years ago over the Christmas holidays, I spent an afternoon indulging in a favorite hobby—shopping for used book. While browsing the shelves of one store, I ran across and purchased a great little book called *Children's Letters to God.* As the title suggests, the book is nothing more than a compilation of real letters from real children addressed to God. Some of the letters made me laugh out loud while others brought tears to my eyes.

One of the sections in the little book deals with children's puzzles, questions, and dilemmas about God and faith. Here are some of my favorites:

"Dear God," writes Jane, "In Sunday School they told us what you do. Who does it for you when you are on vacation?"

"Dear God," says Lucy, "Are you invisible or is that just a trick?"

"Dear God," little Dennis offers, "My Grandpa says you were around when he was a little boy. How far back do you go?"

"Dear God," writes Anita, "Is it true my father won't get in Heaven if he uses his bowling words in the house?" (Hample and Marshall, n.p.)

One of the reasons I like these letters so much is that the children who wrote them were willing to admit something that adults often are not. They had questions for God. In all of their innocence, these little boys and girls were willing to ask their questions openly and freely and say without embarrassment that there were simply some aspects of this faith business that they didn't understand.

Whether or not we are willing to be as honest, all believers, at some point, struggle with an aspect of their faith. Questions of faith may linger throughout our lives, and there is nothing wrong with this reality. As Paul himself said, being a human means "seeing through a glass darkly" (1 Cor 13:12) when it comes to our relationship with God. In fact, one could argue that ongoing faith questions are healthy because they allow us to maintain the proper perspective as we reaffirm that God's ways are beyond our complete comprehension.

The text at the heart of this session provides us with one of the ongoing questions that many Christians have wrestled with over the centuries: Why did Jesus need to be baptized? If the baptism offered by John the Baptist was primarily about the repentance of sins and a turning of one's life toward God, why did Jesus have to go through with it? If Jesus was without sin, what was he repenting of? Such concerns have led to struggles with this text since the beginning of the church.

Jesus' Baptism and the Early Church

It is interesting to read the four Gospels' descriptions of this event. If you read the Gospels in chronological order (based on the dates we believe they were written), you will find that Jesus' baptism takes up less and less space the younger the Gospels become. Here in Mark and also in Matthew, the story is told explicitly. Yet, by the time you get to Luke and John, which are considered to be the youngest of the four Gospels, the story is already beginning to fade. In Luke, the text says Jesus was baptized, but there is no mention that John the Baptist performed the baptism (Luke 3:21-22). In the Gospel of John, the event is alluded to but is never clearly articulated (John 1:29-34). Further still, in the other New Testament works and letters, Jesus' baptism only receives sparse attention. Obviously, this diminished attention must have been related, at least in part, to the early church's increasing discomfort with this event and the complexity of its meaning.

John the Baptist

Before beginning to understand the baptism of Jesus, we must first gain insight into the life and work of the one who ultimately immersed Jesus in the Jordan River, John the Baptizer. According to the Gospels, John and Jesus were related through their mothers, Elizabeth and Mary. Luke tells us that when Mary was pregnant with Jesus, she sought refuge in the home of Elizabeth, who was pregnant with John. Their kinship led Mary to feel safe with Zechariah and Elizabeth. The fact that Elizabeth was pregnant as well surely helped Mary feel that she would find both shelter and compassion in her relative's home.

Beyond being related, Jesus and John were roughly the same age. They also shared a sense of having been set aside from the beginning for God's unique work. Having said this, it may be surprising to some that many scholars doubt Jesus and John knew each other or spent significant time together before the start of Jesus' public ministry, which begins with his baptism. While we can't know for sure, the Gospels do not suggest any relationship between the two prior to Jesus' baptism.

According to Mark and the other Gospels, John, clothed in camel's hair and eating a diet that consisted primarily of locusts and wild honey, lived a unique life in the wilderness. He may have been connected to the Essenes, who also lived in the same region during this time. The Essenes were a separatist religious group within Judaism who saw themselves as being uniquely and solely on God's side. As citizens of this rugged region, they focused on study of the Torah, continuous worship, keeping a proper calendar, ritual washings, and a sacred meal. They also anticipated the arrival of two Messiahs (Trafton, 271–73).

John preached a message of reform while focusing on the coming judgment of God, the need for repentance as a way of preparing oneself for the coming of the Messiah, and the reality that those born of Jewish heritage were not automatically exempt from this judgment simply because of their birth. According to John, they too needed to repent and be baptized as a way of preparing themselves (Chance, 458–59).

John and the Essenes overlapped to a certain degree when it came to John's baptism and the Essene practice of ritual bathing. The idea was that cleansing waters symbolized a desire for spiritual cleansing and refocusing oneself on God. John may have been influenced also by the ritual bathing practiced by Gentiles who desired to convert to Judaism. Here, the act of baptism served as a symbol that one had been purged or cleansed of one's life as a Gentile and was ready to begin anew and fresh as a Jew.

This corresponds with the definition of the term "baptism." When speaking of the meaning of baptism, many believers today are quick to focus on the fact that this Greek word (*baptizo*) means "to dip" or "immerse." While this is true and valuable for discussion, it is a definition more connected with the *mode* rather than the *meaning* of the baptismal act. Thankfully, these are not the only two ways of defining the term. A lesser-known etymology is that "baptism" was also used to describe the destruction of a person by drowning or a ship by sinking. This idea gets at the heart of John's words in Mark, as he calls people to repent, to turn away from an old life and toward an intentional focus on God and God's ways. As Mark 1:4 says, John "proclaimed a baptism of *repentance* for the forgiveness of sins." And people listened. Even though John's call was confrontational and challenging, "people from the whole Judean countryside and all the people of Jerusalem were going out to him, and confessing their sins" (Mark 1:5).

Contextually, this second definition also seems to fit well, not only with what John was saying, but also with what Jesus did. John called for beginning a new life, and Jesus' baptism marked a new chapter in his life with the advent of his public ministry. Again, the idea is that a completely new life was beginning.

The early church maintained this ideology in the fact that baptismal candidates during that time were baptized in the nude. Upon exiting the water, they were given a baptismal robe. These fresh clothes placed on the cleansed body signified that a brand new day had begun in each of their lives (Stookey, 103).

Jesus' Baptism

Most scholars believe that Jesus was roughly thirty years old when he presented himself for baptism at the Jordan. All of the Gospel writers place this event at the beginning of their accounts of Jesus' life, but the story appears the earliest in Mark and John (in the first chapter of each). As has been noted, all four Gospels point to this moment as the beginning of Jesus' public ministry. Starting with his baptism, Jesus' ministry will extend through the region for roughly three years before ending in the crucifixion in Jerusalem.

In Mark, John never explicitly suggests that Jesus should be baptized (v. 9). Instead, it seems John was totally unprepared for this moment and may have needed coaxing to immerse his relative. After all, John was beginning to recognize that this was the one for whom the Baptizer felt unworthy "to stoop down and untie the thongs of his sandals" (Mark 1:7).

There has been much debate about the very moment at which John recognized Jesus as the promised Messiah whose coming he was heralding. Some read the Gospels and conclude that John recognized Jesus' identity before the baptism; some infer he recognized it during the actual event of Christ's baptism; and some believe John did not fully grasp Jesus' true purpose until a later date. Mark is ambivalent on this point. In fact, in Mark 1:11, God's pronouncement that this was the beloved Son with whom God was well pleased seems to be a message to which only Jesus was privy. At least in Mark, it appears that John did not even have this revelation as a means of either further confirming or clarifying his understanding of Jesus' identity.

This moment in Mark resounds with Old Testament imagery that emphasizes that importance of both Jesus *and* John. The description of John echoes that of the prophet Elijah (2 Kings 1:8; Mal 4:5, etc.). In fact, John ultimately would be described as the last of the great prophets in the line of Elijah. Like Elijah, John was identified by his clothing and as someone who proclaimed God's message in a barren wilderness (Dowd, 11).

Similarly, descriptions of Jesus evoke Old Testament prophets such as Isaiah. In Mark, the baptism functioned as a type of anointing scene such as we find in Isaiah 6. Like Isaiah, Jesus hears God's voice in a unique, powerful way. Like Isaiah, Jesus is set apart through this event and begins his public ministry with this very act. Like the vision Isaiah had in the temple, this is the beginning point and the time that all Gospels point back to as the moment it all began (Dowd, 11).

It is important to note that anyone in the Mediterranean world would have recognized the significance of the baptismal scene. In ancient biographies, doves were often pictured in scenes that provided someone's legitimacy. In other words, early followers would have seen in the dove a sign of God's divine favor and blessing (Talbert, 40).

Life Lessons

While questions will always surround the story of Jesus' baptism, this text and this moment in Christ's life have tremendous significance for believers today. Jesus may not have "needed" baptism to have his sins forgiven, but he was interested in identifying with the humanity of John's followers. He also expanded the meaning and intent of this (eventual) holy event for the (eventual) Christian church. For Jesus, baptism became the gateway through which he walked into his public ministry. With wet hands and face as well as muddy toes from the murky Jordan, Jesus introduced to all who would follow him the point at which real life and ministry begin.

Baptism still symbolizes forgiveness of sins and that God through God's spirit has taken up residence in our lives. But that is not all; baptism also symbolizes the beginning of our ministry in the kingdom of God. It is the point from which a lifetime of service, work, and learning in faith has its genesis. This is the point at which the Spirit, like a dove, comes to confirm God's presence in us, God's pleasure with us, and God's willingness to direct our paths. The significance of baptism is thus multifaceted and more complex than its mode or method.

Unfortunately, many individual believers and corporate church bodies have forgotten the many aspects of baptism's meaning. In too many instances, baptism has been relegated to nothing more than a washing away of sins. This single-purpose meaning makes baptism the peak of a mountain after which everything else is downhill. Cleansing sin is obviously important, but baptism is more appropriately understood as a door along the journey of living that leads into a new existence.

All of us have known new "believers" who walked into the baptismal pool only to exit the church doors, dripping wet, never to be seen again. In their lives, baptism signifies that they have provided for themselves some type of eternal security. Their baptism in no way influences God's daily calling on their lives.

William Carter captured this idea a few years ago in a sermon broadcast on the Protestant Hour. Baptism, he said, "is the event that guides the way we live. What matters most is how we live after the water has dried" (Carter).

This is exactly what we find in this early narrative from Mark. Jesus' baptism was certainly a pivotal point in his life and ministry. The reality, though, is that Jesus' actions over the next three years are what ultimately exhibited his understanding of what happened that day in the Jordan. As with us, what happened after the water dried proved to be the most critical stage.

Each morning as I shower, I pray. Generally speaking, I end the prayer with the words "Lord, help me to live today in light of my baptism." In other words, my baptism was my entrance into ministry—not professional ministry, mind you, but rather the ministerial work God calls all believers to do. So, each day, I must ask God for his guidance as I seek to live in light of this calling I received and the commitment I made on that holy and significant day when I followed Jesus' footsteps and entered the water.

In the end, one must say that while baptism does not save us, it certainly does play a central role in the salvation act. On the one hand, as was the case for the Jews to whom John the Baptist preached, baptism symbolizes the work that God has done and continues to do in our lives. On the other hand, baptism also calls us into close community with Christ, as it serves as our entry into the great work of carrying salvation, peace and hope to the world.

1. What is your biggest question about the Gospels? Which text do you struggle with the most? Has Jesus' baptism figured into your difficulties with the New Testament over the years?

_____
_____
_____
_____
_____
_____
_____

2. Do you believe that the early church struggled with the idea of Jesus' being baptized? Why or why not?

Yes Jesus was without Sin and the Messiah ... why did he need his "Sins" washed away.

_____
_____
_____
_____

3. How do you define the term *baptism*? How do this session and your interaction with the focal text change your perspective?

_____
_____
_____
_____
_____
_____

4. How is the idea of baptism reshaped for you through the connection of baptism with death?

_____

_____

_____

_____

_____

_____

5. How do the words of John the Baptist and the insights into baptism in Judaism and the Essene community shape your understanding of Jesus' baptism?

_____

_____

_____

_____

_____

_____

6. How did Jesus' baptism shape his own understanding of God's plans for him? How clearly did Jesus understand his role as God's Son before this event?

_____

_____

_____

_____

_____

_____

7. In what ways does your baptism influence your faith?

_____

_____

_____

_____

_____

_____

8. What aspects of Jesus' baptism are still conveyed in baptismal services today? Which aspects of Jesus' baptism are lost in baptismal services today?

_____

_____

_____

_____

_____

_____

Back to Nature:
The Parable of the Sower

Mark 4:1-20

Several years ago when I was serving in North Carolina, I offered a summer Bible study based on *The Andy Griffith Show*. Each week, we would watch an episode of the show and then spend fifteen or twenty minutes connecting what we had seen with a passage of Scripture. There is nothing novel about such a methodology these days, but, at that time, the study was unique.

I must confess that the idea of paralleling the Scriptures and *The Andy Griffith Show* was not my own; I borrowed the idea from someone else. As luck would have it, though, our study received some local attention and interest while the real originator of the idea and his work were almost completely overlooked. In the process of our study, I received a call from our National Public Radio affiliate, who wanted to interview me about what we were doing. In the course of her questions, she asked, "Why do you think this idea appeals to people?" In my response, I talked about how stories capture people's interest, attention, and imagination. I said that my thought was that television shows for modern Americans are somewhat similar to Jesus' use of parables. We are familiar with the stories, we pay attention to the stories, and we allow them to continue to have some modicum of influence upon our lives long after our first meeting with them. In many instances, we return to them over and over again for months and years beyond the initial encounter.

Despite these attributes, little is known about the origins of Jesus' parables. After all, we don't even know if they were original to Jesus, or if they were stories and statements that he borrowed from others. What we do know, however, is that the parables communicated truths of the kingdom as did no other teaching methodology Jesus employed.

Curiously, while parables played a major role in the overall synoptic picture, they play a minor role in Mark. Most scholars believe that this diminished position is related to Mark's overall perspective—Mark is primarily a Gospel of action. Jesus' concrete deeds are much more prominent in Mark than Jesus' words. That seems to be why Mark focuses on the miracles while seeming to forget the parables. In the end, though, even Mark had to admit that one of the things Jesus did was teach. A few parables do filter into his account—even one that is not found anywhere else in the overall Gospel corpus (the parable of the Growing Seed, Mark 4:26-29). Nowhere do the parables figure more prominently in Mark than in chapter 4, which starts with one of the most familiar of all the parables, Jesus' story of the sower. This parable was deemed so significant that it is retold in each of the Synoptics (Robertson, 95).

What Are Parables, Anyway?

Before getting too carried away with the parable of the Sower, it is important to pause and make sure we have a good grasp of exactly how parables work. Having said this, we must admit that there is much debate and disagreement regarding this subject. The difficulty comes when one realizes that various people view a wide variety of literary styles as parables. While some would say that only "story-like" narratives should be seen as parables, others include short sayings and quips. Still others include in the definition characters and events that serve as an example of something. In other words, one might have no trouble seeing the story of the Good Samaritan as a parable because it is obviously a story that conveys a significant meaning beyond itself. But one might not be so prone to think of Jesus' words about hiding your lamp under a bushel basket in Mark 4:21-23 or the idea that Solomon symbolizes wisdom as also being forms of parables (Long, 87–94).

This all leads to wide disagreement over just how many parables there actually are in the New Testament. An example of this is the fact that in his work *Studies in Mark's Gospel*, A. T. Robertson says that the total number of parables Jesus told in the Gospels is somewhere between twenty-seven and fifty-nine. Again, it depends on what you call a parable (Robertson, 106).

Another question related to parables regards their literary function. Is the hope of parables to clarify things or to leave us doing a bit of guessing? Once more, this depends on which parable you consider. Take Mark 4 again as an example. With the parable of the Sower, verses 13-20 immediately follow the story itself and offer explanation. However, with the parable of the Growing Seed in verses 26-29 of the same chapter, another difficult story is offered with no explanation at all. So which is it? Apparently the answer is both. On the one hand, it seems okay to offer concrete explanations and meanings for the parables we have heard. On the other hand, it is also perfectly fine to see in the parables the desire to leave things somewhat open. This allows our minds to keep thinking and for the possibility that different meanings can be significant and valuable to us at different points in our lives.

How can we clarify this unique literary style? I think C. H. Dodd's well-used definition provides us with a good foundation from which to work:

> At its simplest a parable is a metaphor or simile drawn from nature or common life, arresting the hearer by its vividness or strangeness, and leaving the mind in sufficient doubt about its precise application to tease it into active thought. (Dodd, 16)

While this perspective does not say everything there is to know about parables, nor does it accurately describe all parables, it is still an excellent vantage point from which to explore not only our text for this session but all such Gospel sections that one might label as parabolic.

Farm Fables

Jesus understood the lives of the people he sought to teach. He didn't attempt to employ fantastic stories his listeners couldn't relate to. Instead, appreciating the fact that his was an agrarian society, Jesus centered many of his parables around farming life and the daily rituals of planting, tending, and harvesting. Chapter 4 of Mark is a perfect example: three of its four parables have an agricultural setting. The parable of the Sower, which begins the chapter, illustrates this point well and is likely the most familiar of the three.

One of the first debatable points about this story is how it should be named. If you search the countless studies of these verses, you would find that some people label this the parable of the Soils, and some are prone to remember it as the parable of the Sower (as I have done and will continue to do in this session). Not surprisingly, a solid argument can be made for either of these as a perfectly suitable label. The truth is that in most cases, the title is related to the emphasis or primary meaning given to the story. In other words, for those who find the most meaning in the soil analysis done here, this is the parable of the Soils. For those who find more value in evaluating the behavior of the one who casts the seeds in the story, then this is the parable of the Sower. Despite the fact that Jesus interprets the story in light of the soils more than in light of the sower, either approach to the text is appropriate. It's likely that students of this text may identify with the soil analogies at some points in their faith journey while finding more resonance with the sower's behavior at other points.

The Soils

Interpreting the text as it relates to the soils begins with the recognition that Jesus mentions four types of soil in the story. Along the way, the farmer drops seed onto the compacted, impenetrable soil of the pathway (v. 4), in soil that is rocky (v. 5), in soil that is covered in briars and thorns (v. 7), and finally in soil that is rich and free of impediments (v. 8). In the first three soils, the seed struggles to grow. Upon the path, no growth takes place whatsoever. In the soil hampered by rocks and thorns, at least some degree of development occurs. In the end, all three types of soil lead to situations in which the seed fails to reach its full potential by actually producing a crop. Only the last soil sees growth, and it is of such a nature that the farmer might have been just as shocked by the abundance as he had been disappointed by the previous soil failures.

Traditionally, believers have viewed these soils as illustrative of the various types of people in the world and our responsiveness to the gospel message. Some read the story and ask, "What kind of soil am I? Am I the footpath, the rocky and thorny ground, or the receptive soil?" Others interpret the text as more of a call to recognize that our lives are cyclical; that we will at times be each type of soil but ultimately return to those periods of rich and fertile acceptance.

These are helpful viewpoints and can be valuable to us not only as ways of measuring our own spiritual "soil" but also as ways of understanding that others will be receptive to the gospel "seed" to varying degrees. Not everyone will be rich soil that easily and quickly receives the word of God that we might be trying to sow in their lives. At the same time, not everyone will be thorns and thistles, eager to reject whatever good news we offer.

One temptation these perspectives offer is the enticement to become so fixated on the three types of soil that fail to produce that we miss the value found in the description of the fertile soil. As Kate Moorehead points out in her book *Organic God*, Jesus emphasizes that the fertile soil produced different yields. Some "yielded thirty and sixty and a hundred fold" (v. 9). What Moorehead suggests is that there is a significant lesson here too in the varying degrees of the harvest (Moorehead, 36–38).

Moorehead points out that sometimes we are prone to become disappointed or self-conscious of our own fruitfulness in the kingdom of God when we begin to compare ourselves to others and their spiritual accomplishments. Yet, as Moorehead writes, the important thing is that we are producing, not that we are outdoing everyone else. After all, "the grain produced is worth celebrating, no matter its amount. God celebrates your growth as if you alone were in the universe . . ." (Moorehead, 38).

We must also recognize that Jesus uses this story to touch upon some frank realities of kingdom work. Whether you come at this parable from the point of view of the soil or the sower, you come face to face with some mathematical straight talk. More times than not, the hoped-for harvest does not occur. Only one in four types of soil actually produces. In the same vein, the sower seems to waste a lot of seed. In a refreshing way, Jesus is hopeful and realistic all at the same time. Within the same parable one encounters the hope of an abundant harvest and the everyday truth of failure. The human tendency may be to drift either to unattainable hopefulness or to an attitude of looming failure, yet Jesus seems to call for the need of a happy medium between the two.

The Sower

Soil analysis is only one side of this parable. Just as significant is the sower himself. Who is the sower? Like much else in the parables, that depends on who is interacting with the story and where they are in their lives. The tendency might be to assume that the sower is God and thus focus the story on both God's generosity and again on our receptivity to God's attempts to be at work in our lives. The other option is to identify with the sower and thus allow the story to help us understand our role as lavish sowers of the seeds of the kingdom of God.

Either way, one cannot escape the generous and extravagant way in which the farmer goes about his work. At face value, you get the impression that there is little concern here for where the seed falls. What seems most important is that the seed needs to be scattered. When reading the parable from the point of view of the sower, liberal distribution is the preferred order of the day.

This may be a difficult word to hear. In a world where production, cost, stewardship, and efficiency are buzzwords both in the church and in the larger Western society, the behavior of the sower seems a little unorthodox. Most of us would never think of being so careless or cavalier. Our tendency would be to skip over obvious poor soil so that we might concentrate on ground where maximum growth and maturity would certainly take place. Notice though that in the parable, while Jesus makes it clear that there was good soil and poor soil, we are never told that the sower actually knew how the various soils would perform. What we are told is that he was simply faithful to sowing the seed and comfortable with the mystery of what would eventually happen.

Jesus' Interpretation

Unlike many of the other parables that we encounter in Mark and the Synoptic Gospels, the parable of the Sower ends with Jesus interpreting the passage for his disciples (vv. 14-20). Jesus focuses his thoughts on the soils and the comparison between the ground the seed encounters and the fertile nature of human lives as we encounter the gospel seed of God.

What may be difficult to understand here is not the interpretation that Jesus gives, but that he chooses to interpret the parable (many—if not most—of the parables we encounter in the New Testament are not interpreted). As in C. H. Dodd's definition of parables above, most literature of this type is left unexplained; this way, the hearer can continue to work with, reflect upon, and interact with the story over time. Likewise, this methodology also allows for the meaning of the parable to change and expand as we make our way through the various seasons of life and the spiritual journey.

If this is the way parables generally work, why did Jesus feel a need to explain? Two possibilities seem to be worth our consideration. First, as has already been mentioned, each parable seems to work somewhat differently within the Gospels. As a result, perhaps there simply were times when Jesus felt compelled to provide explanation and clarification to those who heard him as he does here with the disciples. At other times, Jesus' own wisdom may have simply led him to remain silent and allow the hearers to wrestle with the meaning and value on their own.

A second possibility is offered by a number of New Testament scholars who consider the role that the early church played in the construction of the Synoptic Gospels as we have them today. They remind us that the early New Testament church and its leaders inserted their own commentary into the life of Jesus in the Gospels. Furthermore, scholars such as Joachim Jeremias point out that the parables are a common place where the fingerprints of the early church can be found. The parable of the Sower could be one of those texts. In other words, the explanation offered in verses 13-20 may not have originated with Jesus but rather with the early church. From this perspective, it was the early church rather than Jesus who could not resist the temptation to explain the "real" meaning of the parable (Long, 94).

The Apocalyptic Angle

When reading this chapter, the reader is also struck by the similar chord that resounds in each of the three agricultural stories in Mark 4. The parables of the Sower, the Untended Seed, and the Mustard Seed all hint at a common theme. Each of them calls for the realization that in the end there is a positive outcome. In the sower story, the first three soils fail to produce, but the final soil gives a bumper crop. In the parable of the Untended Seed, a crop is produced even while the farmer sleeps and in spite of his inability to comprehend exactly how things have happened. With the mustard seed, the surprise outcome far exceeds any expectation one might have when first glancing at such a small and seemingly insignificant seed.

This common thread is in no way a coincidence. Within Mark as a whole, one of the underlying concerns seems to be persecution being faced by the early church and the fear that believers will turn apostate by renouncing their faith. In light of this, Mark seems to work hard to encourage steadfast belief and a willingness to remain faithful in spite of current conditions or the feeling that progress is not being made. Thus the stories of Mark 4 continually hammer at the idea that while things may seem bleak or "fruitless" in the moment, in the end fruit will appear, signifying and solidifying the worthwhile nature of the early church's labor (Dowd, 43).

The Secret Gospel

One cannot easily let go of the parable of the Sower without momentarily dwelling on Jesus' words in verses 11 and 12 at the transition between the parable itself and Jesus' explanation. In these verses, the reader encounters one of the most difficult sayings of Jesus' ministry as he seems to suggest that one of the purposes of parables is to confuse some people and thus thwart their attempt to understand the gospel message.

While we cannot easily explain away these words, it is helpful to remember the context within which these words were originally spoken. By this point in his ministry, Jesus and his followers were gaining the attention of the religious establishment and the Roman leadership, and both were seeking all opportunities to shut down Jesus' ministry and his message. Perhaps the idea was to talk in such a way that allowed those with sincere motives to hear and understand but prevented those with insincere motives from finding yet another quote or questionable teaching with which to further condemn and attempt to silence the Son of God. Thus the point was not to confuse outsiders in general but rather to prevent those with evil intentions from gaining further ammunition.

Life Lessons

As is the case with almost all of the parables, there are many important life lessons connected to the parable of the Sower. Allow me to focus on two that seem particularly important for us as the church today.

First, God calls us to worry about sowing the gospel seed rather than becoming consumed with analyzing the soil where we sow. We live in a day where fewer and fewer people are receptive to the gospel. This fact alone may cause us to want to throw up our hands and either to refrain from sharing our faith at all or to be cautious as to where we exert our energies and invest ourselves. The parable of the Sower strongly cautions against such an idea. In a profound way, this parable (along with that of the Untended Seed later in this same chapter) reminds us that our kingdom role should not be burdened with trying to decide who is or is not worthy of receiving God's love. Our role is simply to scatter seed abundantly, generously, and lavishly wherever we go.

When I was serving as a pastor in North Carolina, our congregation was involved with Habitat for Humanity. At the time, the

Habitat affiliate we were working with was building an entire neighborhood of homes on a tract of land that had been given to the organization. One Saturday, we learned that the on-site Habitat trailer that was filled with tools and other supplies had been broken into and many items were missing. Over time it began to appear that the culprits were homeowners who were living in houses our affiliate had built. When this news broke, there were those who felt it was time to abandon the project. Ultimately, cooler heads prevailed; we were called to be faithful to the project God had given us to complete. Our task was not dependant on the righteousness of the benefactors. Said another way, our job was to sow seed—not to critique the soil where it was being planted.

Second, collectively the parables of Mark 4 remind us that Christian hope is found in seeing the world not as it is but as it shall be. Just as was the case for the early Christians who encountered this parable, believers through the ages have struggled to maintain faith in the midst of trying and sometimes dark days. It is easy to allow the troubles of today to transform a lifelong trust in God, even if it has always been vibrant and strong. Over and over again in the New Testament, believers are urged to recognize that, despite our current troubles, God will ultimately reign supreme and our lives will be redeemed. This ultimate truth is found in the Revelation, throughout Paul's writings, and also is embedded in this chapter from Mark. This forward-looking hope is a valuable word, whether we are facing persecution, dealing with cancer, or confronting any other life situations that can cloud our faith and call into question our deepest beliefs.

1. How do you define the term *parable*? Which is your favorite parable of Jesus? Why does it speak to you?

_____

_____

_____

_____

_____

_____

2. When you think about the parable that begins Mark 4, are you prone to focus on the soils or the sower? Why?

_____

_____

_____

_____

_____

_____

3. Which type of soil most characterizes your life at this point in your spiritual journey? Why?

_____

_____

_____

_____

_____

_____

4. Are you always a generous sower of gospel seed? If not, what types of soil test your generosity? Why do you struggle to sow abundantly in these areas?

_____

_____

_____

_____

_____

_____

5. Do you think that the church is usually honest about the difficulties associated with sowing kingdom seeds? Why or why not?

_____

_____

_____

_____

_____

_____

6. What do you think Jesus meant when he suggested that he desired for the meaning of this parable to remain hidden from some people?

_____

_____

_____

_____

_____

_____

7. Are you comfortable with the parables remaining unexplained, or are you more at home with concrete guidance as to how a parable should be understood? Explain your perspective.

_____

_____

_____

_____

_____

_____

8. Are there modern parables that have become important stories for the church to return to over and over again today? If so, what are they?

_____

_____

_____

_____

_____

_____

Jesus and the Demoniac

Mark 5:1-20

What defines a miracle? Is it the suspension of the natural order through which God acts? Is it something that is both timely and unexpected that works in favor of someone in need? Does winning the lottery factor in? Obviously the answer depends on who asks, as experts in philosophy, psychology, and theology would certainly give different responses. Webster's dictionary defines a miracle as "an event that seems to contradict scientific laws." Wikipedia, the online information center, goes into much greater detail in defining miracles:

> A miracle is a fortuitous event believed to be caused by interposition of divine intervention by a supernatural being in the universe by which the ordinary course and operation is suspended or modified. In casual usage, miracle may also refer to any statistically unlikely but beneficial event such as survival of a natural disaster.

C. S. Lewis defines a miracle as "an interference with Nature by supernatural power" (5). He goes further in building his unique argument by stating, "Unless there exists, in addition to Nature, something else which we may call the supernatural, there can be no miracles" (5). By following Lewis's line of thought, one would see the sharp contrast between the natural order (of which humanity is a part) and the instigator of the natural order, which in Lewis's mind is God. He does, however, state that there are many who see nothing beyond nature, a group he terms *naturalists*. A naturalist would believe that miracles are possible, but would not assign them to a higher being or supernatural agent. Conversely, Lewis also profiles those who see a higher being at work in miraculous events, and he identifies them as *supernaturalists*. While it is possible to be a supernaturalist and not believe in the one God of the Judeo-Christian faith system, Christian apologists like Lewis focus on the existence and reality of the one supreme God. To C. S. Lewis, William Barclay, and other great apologists of the twentieth century, it is singly this God who is behind the creation of all things and, subsequently, the power behind all miracles.

The Old Testament is filled with accounts of miraculous events attributed to God, or to one of God's assigned agents. Many people are familiar with the miracles performed by or through Moses as he was tasked with leading Israel out of captivity in Egypt. The truly defining miracles of Scripture, however, are those performed by Jesus as depicted in the New Testament Gospel accounts. Each of the "four evangelists," Matthew, Mark, Luke, and John, describe the miracles of Jesus, although each provides a unique take on his supernatural acts. Their perspectives vary because they wrote about the life and teachings of Jesus for different audiences and at different times.

It is commonly held that Mark wrote first, followed by Matthew, Luke, and, much later, John. Their versions of the life and actions of Jesus were uniquely propelled by their varying levels of association with Jesus. Where John was a close disciple who witnessed each stage of Jesus' ministry life, Mark was not one of the twelve disciples, nor did he ever travel with Jesus. His depictions of Jesus were handed down to him over time, and that reality shaped the essence of his writings. He did not write as an eyewitness would (or could), thus his Gospel is more of a compiled general assessment that provides a valuable secondary source of the life and work of Jesus. It is also possible that Mark's depictions of Jesus are the most balanced because he wasn't writing to a necessarily religious audience, nor was he interjecting himself into the narrative.

Mark provides a "full-service" accounting and portrayal of Jesus in his short writing. According to James McGowan, "The supernatural power of Christ is copiously displayed in the eighteen miracles noted in Mark, yet his humanity is emphasized as well" (6). This statement is especially true when contrasting Mark to the other Gospel writers. Where Matthew writes as a Jew to other Jews, and John focuses almost exclusively on the divine nature of Jesus, Mark finds a way to craft the "total" Jesus, simultaneously both human and divine.

The Eighteen Miracles in Mark

Removing an evil spirit (1:23-26)

Healing Simon Peter's mother (1:30-31)

Healing a leper (1:40-42)

Healing a paralytic (2:3-12)

Healing a shriveled hand (3:1-5)

Calming the stormy sea (4:37-39)

Healing the Gerasene demoniac (5:2-13)

Healing a hemorrhaging lady (5:25-34)

Raising Jarius's daughter from the dead (5:22-43)

Feeding the five thousand (6:41-44)

Walking on water (6:48-51)

Removing an evil spirit (7:25-30)

Healing a deaf person (7:32-35)

Feeding the four thousand (8:2-8)

Healing a blind person (8:22-26)

The transfiguration (9:2-8)

Removing an evil spirit (9:17-27)

Healing blind Bartimaeus (10:46-52)

These eighteen miracles allow for us to see the absolute power of Jesus as he strikes a blow against sin, sickness, demons, the natural order, human hunger, and death. It is also through these intense displays of power that we see God's foundational love at work within each miracle.

The culture of that time was unduly influenced by magic and superstition. Many contemporary itinerant teachers worked tricks into their acts and were well known for their flash and pizzazz. It is possible that Jesus performed miracles out of perfunctory requirement due to these charlatans. His miracles were obviously more than tricks to keep up with the competition, however, as he demonstrated power that could only be supernatural. Since the supernatural can be defined from the direction of both supreme good and evil, Jesus' miracles were bathed in all things positive. There were no miraculous deeds that led to enhanced position and power for Jesus; in fact, his work led to his being first shunned and later executed. Through these miracles Jesus proclaimed that he was God and that a new opportunity for salvation had become available to the world. Through these miracles Jesus proclaimed that the vagaries of this life held no power over his love and sovereignty.

Through these miracles Jesus proclaimed that "the Kingdom of God was no longer a distant hope but a dawning reality" (Hunter, 94).

Mark records the first miracle of Jesus in the first chapter of his Gospel account. Jesus is teaching in the synagogue in Capernaum when a person possessed by an evil spirit cries out, "What do you want with us, Jesus of Nazareth? Have you come to destroy us? I know who you are—the Holy One of God!" (1:24). Jesus casts out the demon with the command "Come out of him." Mark records that those in attendance were amazed at the power and authority of Jesus and news began to spread of his "new" teaching.

Soon after leaving the synagogue, Jesus and his new disciples visit the home of Simon and Andrew where they find Simon's mother-in-law in bed with a high fever. Jesus heals her by taking her hands and lifting her from the sick bed. She instantly recovers from her fever and straightaway begins to serve them. Later that evening, people hoping to be cured by Jesus gather at Simon and Andrew's family home. Mark records that many were healed of diseases and from demon possession. It is interesting to note that many of Jesus' early miracles centered on releasing people from demon possession. This is a difficult concept for today's modern reader as demon possession has been relegated to the level of horror movie or serial novel. If Mark and the other Gospel writers are correct, however, demon possession was indeed a facet of life in this era.

The Gerasene Demoniac

Jesus' signature encounter with demon possession is recorded in Mark 5. Jesus and the disciples had sought refuge from the burgeoning crowds of the curious and needy by crossing a body of water. They set out in the evening and while en route encountered a storm that sent waves over the sides of the boat. In the midst of this storm Jesus was sleeping in the stern of the boat. The frightened disciples woke him and asked, "Teacher, don't you care if we drown?" (4:38). Jesus stood up and commanded the unruly waves to become still. The forces of nature obeyed Jesus and the waters and winds calmed. He chastised his disciples over their continuing lack of faith. They proved his assessments correct as they asked each other, "Who is this? Even the wind and the waves obey him" (4:41). Little did they know that an even greater feat of power awaited them on the Gentile side of the lake.

Upon their arrival, a naked man charged toward Jesus and his disciples. The man wore the remnants of shackles and was living among the tombs, a sure sign that he was either mad or under the control of evil spirits. Any person who exhibited signs of demon possession was excluded from normal society and restricted to the areas already deemed as unclean. In the case of some, however, the exclusions were temporary as these individuals also took on superhuman strength. It is likely that this person, commonly known as the Gerasene Demoniac, had been bound with chains and shackles but had broken free and literally roamed wild. Scottish theologian William Barclay writes that demon possession was ingrained into the superstitious culture of that era:

> The belief of the intermingling of the human and the divine showed itself in the belief of demon possession. Men believed that the air and atmosphere were crowded with demons, most of them malignant spirits waiting to work men harm. The most common explanation for their existence was that they were the offspring and descendants of the wicked angels, who in the old story descended from heaven and seduced mortal women (Genesis 6:1-8). It was believed that they could eat and drink, that they could begat children, and so propagate their own evil line. All illness was ascribed to these demons. (*The Mind of Jesus*, 72–73)

There is little doubt that this man was his village's *boogeyman*. Mark's descriptions create the illusion of a tormented soul so violated by physical, mental, and spiritual illness that he was a danger both to himself and to those with whom he came into contact. The fact that he lived among the caves and tombs, long seen as the natural abode of demons and evil creatures, reinforces Mark's portrayal that he was controlled by demons. And while it appears true that no one could control this man, Jesus had an immediate effect on him. Theologically this is a salient point for defining the parameters of Jesus as the God/Man who came to usher in God's kingdom. That Jesus simply stepped onto dry land and attracted a demon-possessed person speaks volumes to the innate power of Jesus and God's ultimate power over evil. David E. Garland sums it up this way: "Wherever Jesus goes, his holy presence, like some chemical catalyst, triggers an immediate reaction from the unholy" (202).

The Encounter

Upon seeing Jesus, the demon-possessed man ran toward him and fell prostrate at his feet. It appears that the man was, at some level, frightened of Jesus. Immediately before touching the eastern shore of the lake, the disciples were also afraid of Jesus—but for much different reasons. The demoniac was afraid of the presence of God standing over him. To this end, the demons even declared who Jesus is: "What do you want with me, Jesus the Son of the Most High God? Swear to God that you won't torture me!" (5:7).

The demons declared the full divinity of Jesus, and in so doing stated a theological fact heretofore lost on the disciples: "You are the Son of God." It is thought by many scholars that this outward acknowledgment by the demons would or could bind the power of Jesus over them. However, just as was the case in James 2:19 ("Even the demons believe and shudder"), this was a supreme mismatch. Edwards believes "that the emphasis here falls not on exorcism *per se* but on Jesus subduing the demon world into his authority" (104). If this assessment is correct, it may answer why demonic possession lessened over time.

Jesus chose to speak with the demon host controlling the man. "What is your name?" "My name is Legion," he replied, "for we are many" (5:9). Customarily the Roman word *legion* defined the largest military unit, one that consisted of up to six thousand soldiers. Those who would like to know the exact number of demons inhabiting this man will be disappointed, for the word simply denotes a large number. These demons were a surly bunch as well: in verse 8 Jesus commands them to come out of the man, but they resist and begin a dialogue. Many scholars see this episode as a large block of powerful demons attempting to trick Jesus into not destroying them. The *Life Application Bible Commentary* on Mark provides a more literal translation of the question put forth by the demons:

> A more literal translation of Mark 5:7 would be "What to you and to me," or "What do we have in common?" In other words, the demon asked Jesus to leave them alone, for they had nothing to do with each other. Such a question and statement show the demons' ultimate rebellion. Jesus and the demons were as far separated as anything could be. Why did Jesus allow the demons to speak at all? Some scholars believe this was done to set the scene for Jesus' revelation of overwhelming power over the demons. (Barton et al., 129).

It seems certain that these savvy and powerful demons did use trickery and deception in dealing with Jesus. By speaking first, using

God's name, and falling in front of him, the demons tried to control Jesus. In this culture, knowing and stating an adversary's whole name and any titles were believed to provide certain advantage over an opponent. This would be especially true if the person held noble position. Certainly the demons were not citing Jesus' divinity out of respect; they simply sought to take advantage of the noblest aspects of God's love and mercy. This ploy did not work, however; the power of Jesus could not be controlled by even the strongest cadre of evil spirits.

The Exorcism

It is taught that the final destination of all demons will be the pit or abyss (Luke 8:31; Rev 20:10). Matthew 12:43 states, "When an unclean spirit goes out of a man, it goes through dry places, seeking rest, and finds none." These demons seem to be open to any option short of perpetual restlessness or the proverbial final stop. Seeing that the tactics were not working on Jesus, the demons began to beg for mercy: "And he begged Jesus again and again not to send them out of the area" (5:10). There are more opinions than real answers as to what this request means. Evans and Richards believe that the demons knew enough theology to realize that the reign of God's kingdom had begun and their demise was looming (93). It was commonly believed in Gentile areas that demons were territorial and would stay in one area if possible. With their options dwindling and fearing being sent into the demon netherworld, they asked Jesus for a favor.

They begged Jesus again and again not to send them out of the area. A large herd of pigs was feeding on the nearby hillside. The demons begged Jesus, "Send us among the pigs; allow us to go into them." He gave them permission, and the evil spirits came out and went into the pigs. The herd, about two thousand in number, rushed down the steep bank into the lake and were drowned (5:10-13).

The Aftermath

This story certainly captures a lot of action in a short time! To recap, Jesus and his band of twelve crossed the Sea of Galilee and landed on the Gentile area on the east side. As they made landfall, a crazed, naked man came running toward them. His behavior made it apparent that he was under the control of demons. The man fell at the feet of Jesus and called him by name and title. A supernatural sparring match took place, but in the end Jesus sent the demons into a nearby herd of pigs. This event caused the herd of two thousand swine to rush off the nearby cliff and drown in the water below.

Obviously this series of events caused quite a stir in the surrounding areas. It wasn't every day that a famous teacher and miracle worker came to town, especially a Gentile town, and cured the local demoniac. It was also likely that a swine owner lost two thousand pigs in the only reported case of Sudden Onset Demon Possession Swine Disorder. This was a story that begged to be told, and in short order the word was out.

As curiosity seekers converged into the area, they found the man formerly filled with demons sitting peacefully with Jesus. Their first and lasting response to this sight was fear. Never mind that the former scourge of their town had regained his faculties, was properly dressed, and appeared to be normal. Never mind that they had witnessed a battle between supernatural forces and had seen the absolute power firsthand. They were witness to the vanquishing of evil forces and the complete restorative powers of God. Nevertheless, they were afraid, and there were two thousand dead pigs in the water. They had seen more than they were willing to comprehend.

In a sad twist, the demons requested to stay in the area while the townspeople requested that Jesus leave. The final picture is not right, but it is intensely human. There are scholars who believe that the locals could not see beyond their own financial loss of the swine, while others see them as pagans who did not want to upset their gods. It is also possible that as Gentiles they were not yet ready to understand the reality of Jesus as Son of God. It is certain that Jesus coming as the Hebrew Messiah would have been completely lost on them. There was one among them who did not want Jesus to leave, however, and he did have an appreciation of the divinity of Jesus.

The man formerly known as Legion begged Jesus for permission to join the disciples on the boat. Was he fearful of how his own people would treat him? Was he worried about being made the scapegoat for the loss of the swine, or did he become a believer in Jesus and want to become a companion? While there had to be some level of fear about his impending social status, the man appears to have had a genuine encounter with the God of salvation and restoration. Jesus seems to have believed that the man's encounter was real, but Jesus turned down the man's request to go with him. In refusing him, Jesus essentially turned him loose and told him to tell his family all the things that the Lord had done for him. Years later the area known as the Decapolis became home to the burgeoning Christian church. And to think it all began with a demon-possessed man. God does work in mysterious ways.

Life Lessons

A close study of Jesus in Scripture provides a portrait of God in action. Jesus was on a mission, and at every stop he met the needs of the sick or disenfranchised. We know that only a portion of Jesus' story was recorded, so one can only imagine the number of miraculous acts he performed over his three-year ministry. Jesus was all about miracles, and his miracles were all about God. God's restorative grace permeated each one. Many people were healed of disease, some were brought back to life, and others experienced an exorcism of evil spirits. And the goal seems to be twofold: first, a person was healed from a malady that made life difficult; second, God's power was on display. For the people of that day, seeing *was* believing. This was especially true of those who witnessed the healing of Legion and the resulting swine fiasco. A person was miraculously healed and made whole. This was the second-greatest *before* and *after* commercial for God's power and grace of all time. And it was too much for the local Gentiles to deal with.

Perhaps the greatest lesson for the modern reader pertains to God's absolute power over evil. Evil spirits exist in our world just as they did in the time of Legion. Evil people exist in our world just as they have throughout history. The world isn't a safe place, but it never has been. Bad things happen to both good people and bad people. And at the end of the day, God remains sovereign and in power. We may not understand why evil continues to prevail or why the world seems to be declining at light speed, but it's clear that ours is not to reason why. Our job is to proclaim all that God has done in our lives, to shed the light of God onto a dark world, to do what Jesus left the reformed demoniac to do . . . tell our good news to the world.

1. How would you define a miracle to someone who is unfamiliar with the Jesus story?

_____

_____

_____

_____

_____

_____

2. List three miracles performed by Jesus. How are they similar? How are they different?

_____

_____

_____

_____

_____

_____

3. What is the significance of Jesus' being on the other side of the lake in Gentile territory?

_____

_____

_____

_____

_____

_____

4. Describe the state and demeanor of the demon-possessed man as he ran to Jesus.

_____

_____

_____

_____

_____

5. Contrast the man's "possessed" state with the description Mark provides for him after his healing.

_____

_____

_____

_____

_____

_____

6. Why did the demons converse with Jesus as they did?

_____

_____

_____

_____

_____

7. Why did Jesus grant their wish to be sent into the herd of swine?

_____

_____

_____

_____

_____

8. If you had been a Gentile who witnessed this miracle, how would you have reacted? What if you had been the owner of the pigs?

_____

_____

_____

_____

_____

9. What did Jesus leave the man to do after denying his request to go with the disciples?

_____

_____

_____

_____

_____

_____

10. What is a one-sentence conclusion from this story for today's believer?

_____

_____

_____

_____

_____

_____

Blind Familiarity:
Jesus in His Hometown

Mark 6:1-6

The Coalwood Way is Homer Hickam's sequel to the wildly popular book *October Sky*, which was made into a feature film in the late 1990s. The early pages of the novel take the reader to Stephens Clinic Hospital in the county seat town of Welch, West Virginia, where Hickam was born the second child of Homer Sr. and his wife, Elsie. Upon seeing his newborn son, Homer Sr. exclaims, "Elsie, that has got to be the ugliest baby that I have ever seen." With those words, the new father leaves the room. At that moment, Elsie, who has a wry sense of humor, knows that the only name for her boy is Homer Hickam Jr. (Hickam, 17).

Although the origin of Homer Jr.'s name is humorous, the consequences ultimately would be burdensome. Throughout his childhood, Homer preferred the nickname "Sonny" over his given name. Even so, everyone in town knew him as Homer Jr. Part of the reason was the fact that Homer Sr. was the foreman of the Coalwood, West Virginia, coal mine, and Coalwood was a coal mine company town. All life in Coalwood revolved around the mine, and much of life thus centered on Homer Sr. Most people in town believed one day Homer Jr. would replace Homer Sr. in the mines, and evidently Homer Sr. hoped so as well.

Homer Jr. did not share his father's dream or his town's expectation. In fact, not only did he prefer the name "Sonny," but he also loved the nickname "Rocket Boy." Sonny's dream for his life had nothing to do with the mines; instead, he dreamed of leaving Coalwood to pursue his desire of becoming a NASA rocket scientist. Sonny's teenage years became a struggle between father and son. Over and over again, Sonny fought off the expectations associated with being his father's namesake and the eerie call of the Coalwood mine. He grasped for every chance to leave Coalwood and reach for the stars.

In the beginning of Mark 6, we encounter a parallel story. The setting there is the Israelite city of Nazareth rather than Coalwood, West Virginia. Nonetheless, in Nazareth, Jesus faces a dilemma similar to the one that Sonny faced in Coalwood. In the scene, Jesus has just begun his public ministry. His power, wisdom, and actions have reverberated all the way back to the citizens of his hometown. Yet, no matter how much significance the greater Israelite society seems to be placing on Jesus' young shoulders, those who know him best cannot let go of their intimate knowledge of the one who stood before them. Some might want to proclaim him as the promised Messiah, but for the locals, Jesus is still known as Mary's son.

This hauntingly realistic yet tragic moment from the life of Jesus sheds much light on our human predisposition toward judging people based upon where they come from rather than who they have become. It also clarifies why we so easily miss God's presence in our midst. It certainly doesn't take much imagination to understand fully and clearly why prophets are not accepted or listened to in their hometowns!

The Great Difficulty of Being Known . . .

According to verse 2, the setting for this scene is the synagogue in Nazareth. Not merely a place of worship, the local synagogue also served as a schoolhouse and a community center. As a result, in all likelihood, Jesus' presence there meant that he was returning to the place were he had worshiped, was educated, and participated in the everyday events of life within the local community. Despite the power of his teaching, those listening on this particular Sabbath could not get beyond their familiarity with this one who stood before them.

Within the course of only one sentence found in verse 3, the synagogue crowd conveys the essence of how their knowledge of Jesus has become their highest hurdle rather than their greatest help in accepting the message proclaimed. "Is not this the carpenter, the son of Mary and the brother of James and Joses and Judas and Simon, and are not his sisters here with us?"

THE CARPENTER

The first term that the Nazareth locals use to describe Jesus in verse 3 is *tekton* or carpenter. Interestingly, in most texts associated with

Jesus and his family, it is Jesus' earthly father who is referred to as a carpenter. The idea that Jesus was also a carpenter comes from the inference that he followed in the family business. This is the one time in the New Testament where he is explicitly connected to the occupation (Culpepper, 189).

Carpentry as a profession was not necessarily an age-old practice in ancient Israel. People of the period generally took care of their own simple carpentry needs. Further, when major building projects occurred in Israel, such as the building of Solomon's temple or David's residence, carpenters were brought from outside Israel. It seems possible that the type of skilled labor necessary for such work was not available in Israel at the time (Duckat, 42–44).

By the period of Jesus' ministry in Nazareth, carpentry was emerging as a significant trade in the area. In fact, Nazareth would have been an important place for carpenters to reside since the nearby town of Sepphoris was being transformed into an important regional capital within the Roman Empire. Most believe that if Jesus did work regularly as a carpenter, it would have likely been on the many building projects underway in Sepphoris (Culpepper, 189).

The people at the synagogue derided Jesus as a carpenter, but it's not entirely clear what they were insinuating. It does not appear that carpentry as an occupation carried any negative connotations at the time (as did shepherding or working for the Roman government as a tax collector). On the other hand, there is also no evidence that carpentry would have been considered a likely choice for an educated or important figure. Their statement may have been simple ambivalence. The point may have been to ask, "What is so important about a carpenter?" Or, "why would God choose a carpenter as the Messiah?"

THE SON OF MARY

The most derogatory of the comments leveled at Jesus by those in the synagogue that day seems to be their statement that he was "the son of Mary." Rather than identifying Jesus as "the son of Joseph" as would have been more customary during that time, Jesus is associated with his mother. The reason for this has nothing to do with the notion that Jesus was the Son of God. Nor does it seem to be that this was a way of indicating that Jesus' earthly father, Joseph, had died. Much more likely is the sentiment that the question of Jesus' real father was open for debate.

In spite of the holy aura that surrounds the birth of Jesus in the modern church, the event had to have been regarded as scandalous in Jesus' hometown. Certainly few if any in Nazareth actually believed Mary's story that an angel had visited her or that she was the mother of God's child. Instead, the common belief would have likely been that Jesus was merely illegitimate. Either he was Joseph's son and had been conceived out of wedlock, or he was really the son of someone else in the area and Joseph had simply felt pity on Mary and gone through with the marriage despite her betrayal.

Calling Jesus "Mary's son" may have also been a way of identifying his own insanity with hers. In other words, she thought she was the mother of God's child and, like a chip off the old block, Jesus believed he was the Messiah too. To the discerning people of Nazareth, both Mary and Jesus were caught up in a fantasy world that certainly could not have been based on fact. If these events were being played out in our own day, we might be tempted to say "craziness ran in the family."

THE BROTHER OF JAMES, JOSES, JUDAS, AND SIMON

Scholars have long debated the question of Jesus' siblings. Were they the children of Joseph from a previous marriage? Were they the children of relatives who simply came to live in the home of Mary and Joseph for one reason or other? Or did Mary and Joseph have children in the normal fashion in the years after Jesus' birth? No one really knows, and honestly those questions are academic. Likewise, they are of little importance in regard to our text for this session. The more important question is what they meant in light of the people's rejection of Jesus in the Nazareth synagogue (Culpepper, 190).

As good a guess as any is that naming Jesus' siblings was simply a way of connecting him with normal people who did normal things. Remember that the local synagogue was a place for worship, a school, and a community center. This means that just as Jesus likely grew up there, so did his siblings. Nazareth was little more than a bump in the road. It would have been a place where everyone knew each other well, so those who rejected Jesus that day not only knew him well, but they also knew the members of his family well too. They could have simply been saying that they knew James, Joses, Judas, and Simon, and in knowing them they also knew Jesus. If James, Joses, Judas, and Simon were ordinary people who lived life and made mistakes just like everyone else in the Nazareth community, how could Jesus be any different?

In his commentary on Luke's parallel description of this same event, Fred Craddock calls the response to Jesus in Nazareth "blind familiarity." Because they were so familar with Jesus' family, upbringing, and the daily activities of his life, they were blind to the wondrous word of God that Jesus desired to share with them. He was a carpenter for goodness sake; he was Mary's son, and he was the brother of James, Joses, Judas, and Simon—he couldn't be the Messiah. He may have seemed smart, spoken articulately, and displayed a certain degree of power and charisma, but they knew him and thus knew better (Craddock, 63–63).

Where Does the Power Come From?

Despite the fact that their familiarity with Jesus caused the people of Nazareth to question his claims to be the promised Messiah, they still recognized that there was something different and special about the way he taught and conducted himself. This sentiment is conveyed in verse 2: "Where did this man get all this? What is this wisdom that has been given to him? What deeds of power are being done by his hands!"

There are two ways to interpret this section of the passage. One possibility is that the people's initial reaction to Jesus was positive. As they listened to what he said and watched what he did, their hearts told them that he should be believed and followed. But, when they began to think about his occupation and family (v. 3), their heads told them the emotions of their hearts had to be wrong. No matter how good his words sounded or how powerful his deeds were, they knew him and therefore must dismiss his claims (Williamson, 114).

The other possibility is that these statements reveal the dual world within Jewish spirituality at the time. Israelite people believed that every world event as well as every human action had a supernatural cause behind it. This meant that the things that happened in the world were either the work of God or the work of the demonic forces that opposed God. This belief system is implicit within the statements recorded here as the Nazareth populace communicated the feeling that some other-worldly power was behind Jesus' power.

Since they were convinced that Jesus was not of God, they only had one option left. The abilities that Jesus exhibited had to be the result of demonic forces. This perspective may be hard for us to understand in light of the fact that Mark has already told us that Jesus was busy casting out evil spirits. After all, why would one controlled by an evil spirit be working against similar evil? Whether the people in Nazareth were unaware of these deeds or simply chose to ignore them, we do not know. In the end, the Nazareth citizens' associating Jesus with evil may have hurt him more than their blind familiarity in this dark moment in his life (Culpepper, 188–89).

Only Able to Do a Few Miracles

Two difficult verses end this section: " . . . he could do no deed of power there, except that he laid his hands on a few sick people and cured them. And he was amazed at their unbelief" (vv. 5-6). Upon first reading, verse 5 seems to be a complete contradiction. Curing sick people is not a miracle, not a "deed of power"?

The key may be found in the people's attitude toward Jesus in Nazareth. Throughout the passage, they affirm the power and uniqueness of Christ on the one hand while denying his divinity and claim to be the Messiah on the other. They affirm that he is special, but this power is not enough to sway them to follow him. Their hearts say one thing, but their heads quickly get them back on the "right" course. In other places, the faith of those who barely knew Jesus was extraordinary, but no matter how hard he tried, he would never convince the people of his hometown. He did, however, seem to understand human nature when he said in verse 4, "prophets are not without honor, except in their hometown, and among their own kin, and in their own house." As Fred Craddock noted, blind familiarity may just be among the greatest of hurdles to overcome. Sometimes, those we know best are the hardest for us to believe and trust. If verse 4 is taken literally, this may have been the case with not only the citizens of Jesus' town but even many of the members of his own family!

Life Lessons

Many obstacles stand in our way when it comes to believing. This is true whether belief is related to our relationship with God or we are seeking to place our faith in others. This sad yet significant scene of Jesus in his hometown centers on several reasons why belief is so difficult and addresses the same faith struggles we wrestle with today.

First, we learn from this scene that familiarity can be a curse when it comes to faith. Just as the people in Nazareth had difficulty believing Jesus because of how well they knew him, we too sometimes struggle to believe in or accept the claims of others because we know them (and their lives) too well. While we expect others to believe us and to trust us in spite of our past failures or missteps, we generally falter when it comes to offering this same courtesy to others. Just as the crowd in Nazareth, we are quick to point out that we know someone's family, we remember their childhood, or we know how they spend their time. Too often, our knowledge of these characteristics becomes our rationale for our unbelief. This is true of human nature whether we are speaking of having faith in others in general or believing someone's claims about what God is doing in their lives.

This is altogether more tragic in light of the calling of the Scriptures that say God can use us to do amazing things in spite of our past. Indeed, there is hardly a biblical character used by God who did not bring some type of baggage into the situation. Likewise, the biblical record also teaches us that God often calls ordinary, everyday figures to fulfill the most significant tasks of the kingdom. Many times, the very characteristics that would impede our faith are seen by God as ingredients needed for future service.

Second, this text also teaches that sometimes we must follow our hearts rather than our heads when it comes to believing. This is not to suggest that there is no place for reason, intelligence, or rational thinking in our lives of faith. Rather, this text provides a simple reminder that faith cannot be built upon rational thought alone. This is the reason that we call it Christian *faith* rather than Christian *fact*. Belief necessitates that sometimes we must set aside what logic suggests in order to follow where God leads. In a world where we want to understand everything, we must also allow for mystery if we are to be all that God wants us to be.

Third, Jesus' rejection in his hometown reminds us that faith and family don't always go together. A painful reality for many people of faith is that their families cannot embrace or accept the faith to which they are so devoted. Our families know us intimately and thus sometimes struggle to believe what God is doing with and in our lives just as Jesus' own family struggled to accept what was happening in his life.

This does not mean we can't share our faith effectively with our families. To the contrary, we *can* have a profound effect. But we can take heart in realizing that if Jesus struggled to point those who knew him best toward the work of God in their midst, then we should not be surprised when the same difficulties exist in our lives.

1. When have you struggled to believe or put faith in the claims of a close friend or family member?

_____

_____

_____

_____

_____

_____

2. When have you been rejected by close friends or family? How did you feel in that moment? How does that memory help you to identify with Jesus' feelings in this passage?

_____

_____

_____

_____

_____

_____

3. Had you been present in the Nazareth synagogue, which of the concerns leveled would have worried you the most? Why?

_____

_____

_____

_____

_____

_____

4. What does the term "blind familiarity" mean? When have you seen this principle being played out in your own life?

_____

_____

_____

_____

_____

_____

5. Do you struggle more with following your heart or your mind? Which do you tend to see as most important?

_____

_____

_____

_____

_____

_____

6. How do faith and reason coexist for you? Is this a difficult partnership for you?

_____

_____

_____

_____

_____

_____

7. Have you struggled to win family members and close friends to faith? If so, how do Jesus' own struggles help you deal with these difficulties?

_____

_____

_____

_____

_____

8. Do you remember a time when someone placed faith in you when others may have been skeptical? Did they receive criticism for their belief?

_____

_____

_____

_____

_____

The Great
Fish Sandwich Lesson

Mark 6:30-44

The feeding of the five thousand is one of the miracles of Jesus that is most familiar to us. Children learn this story in Vacation Bible School, and even the nominally religious tend to know it. That said, this is also a miracle sequence that is greatly misunderstood—or at best undervalued—by modern readers. It is easy to leap over the symbolism when looking at the larger aspects of this epic "Jesus" event. For many, this is simply a story about a multitude who had traveled a long distance to hear Jesus teach. Jesus was already famous for his teaching and healings and drew huge crowds wherever he went, even in the Gentile areas. In this particular instance, Jesus and his disciples were trying to move away from the masses so they could rest and restore themselves. Jesus' popularity was such that a trip to a new region didn't stop a large group of would-be listeners from gathering and demanding that he teach them:

> The apostles gathered around Jesus and reported to him all they had done and taught. Then, because so many people were coming and going that they did not even have a chance to eat, he said to them, "Come with me by yourselves to a quiet place and get some rest." So they went away by themselves in a boat to a solitary place. But many who saw them leaving recognized them and ran on foot from all the towns and got there ahead of them. When Jesus landed and saw a large crowd, he had compassion on them, because they were like a sheep without a shepherd. So he began teaching them many things. (Mark 6:30-34)

Teaching was a centerpiece of Jesus' ministry and more times than not it was extemporaneous and spontaneous. Chapter 10 of Mark's account opens with, "Jesus then left that place and went into the region of Judea and across the Jordan. Again crowds of people came to him, and as was his custom, he taught them" (v. 1). He met the needs of the people who were drawn to him and took many opportunities to proclaim that God's kingdom had arrived. In the temporal sense, this was both new and confusing news for the average person, especially for Gentiles who held no expectations for a messiah.

The Jews were expecting a messiah, but not one who lacked political aspirations and who was born in the boonies. First-century Palestine was rife with negative factions within Judaism and a hatred of strict Roman rule. These factors combined to make Jesus and his message simultaneously loved and hated through the region. Sadly, the most "religious" Jews were primarily the segment who summarily rejected Jesus as their long-awaited Messiah. Because he didn't fit any of the profiles held by the Hebrew religious community, Jesus' grass roots popularity with the common people was problematic and ultimately attracted the attention of Rome.

In *Who Is This Jesus?*, Michael Green describes the Palestinian region of the early first century as being politically insignificant and under the control of a minion for Rome. Herod the Great was the half-Gentile, half-Hebrew leader of the Jewish territories who served as a "client-king" for Caesar Augustus and Rome. Herod was loyal to Rome and kept his territories stable, even if it meant being cruel to his own people. Jesus was born in the later days of his reign. Much changed in the region over the first thirty years of Jesus' life as Roman rule became localized and the kingship shifted to a local "procurator" who answered to Caesar. As Jesus grew up, he no doubt became accustomed to the sight of Roman troops and an occupied Judea. This tense state of occupation and forced allegiance to Rome spawned the radical Zealot movement, a Hebrew group who fought against all things Roman. The diametrically opposite group was the Sadducees, a politically savvy group of wealthy landowners and priests who acquiesced to Rome out of self-interest and self-preservation. The Sadducees made up the majority of the local counsel, the "Sanhedrin," a group of seventy-one leaders who had limited power in Galilee. The other group in this potentially explosive mix was the Pharisees, a hyper-legalistic sect of Jews who awaited a messiah-king who would overthrow Rome and allow for them to lead the region (Green, 16–18).

By this point, Rome had conquered the known world and had adopted a unique maintenance mode. Through their vast conquests they had created a safe, effective, and fast system of travel and commerce and created a world economy centered in Rome. The fact that Rome had virtually outgrown the known world and had few remaining options for expansion created a tension that resulted in a myopic focus on order and stability throughout the empire. This tension filtered down into every nook and cranny and left the occupied territories with a feeling of fear and doubt about the future. This is the tumultuous world into which Jesus proclaimed his message of God's kingdom, salvation, and peace. A large segment of the common people resonated on his words, but the professional Jews, the Sadducees and the Pharisees, railed against him, albeit for different reasons.

There was another group that figured into the Jesus story in the first century. Their numbers were small, and they didn't make history until after Jesus' death. These men were the original apostles, sometimes referred to as disciples, who numbered but twelve. They weren't flashy, popular, overly educated, or obviously talented. They were common, much like the average person who opted to believe in Jesus as Messiah. They were also slow learners. Scripture consistently cites examples when they missed the point and were confused by the teachings of Jesus. Sometimes referred to as the *duh-ciples*, this group had been sent on a test journey by Jesus and had just returned when the need to feed the large group presented itself. They had been given power to cast out demons and to heal the sick; they had seen Jesus do the same many times, yet they didn't really understand Jesus when they were faced with feeding a crowd of approximately twelve thousand people (including women and children [Matt 14:21]). Obviously none of the twelve came from a catering background, and they hadn't fully grasped that they were hanging around with God Incarnate.

Jesus faced direct opposition from both the Hebrew elite and Rome, and by necessity had to develop his twelve assistants slowly. Did the Roman issues or the opposition from the Hebrew leadership slow his progress? Did the *duh-ciples* require so much time for care and feeding that Jesus couldn't concentrate on the many jobs at hand? It would be difficult to prove either assertion by using the scriptural record. Jesus was busy being Jesus and doing the things that only Jesus could do; including whipping up a last-minute meal for five thousand men and their families . . . *yum-o!*

Feeding the Crowd

The feeding of the five thousand is the only miracle performed by Jesus that is recorded in all four Gospels. In a separate section Mark reports that Jesus fed an assembled group of four thousand people, prompting some to wonder if this type of event happened multiple times or, possibly, not at all. A close study of the language differences within each account sheds light on the similar events. The feeding of the five thousand is told from a uniquely Jewish view, while the story of the four thousand uses language particular to a Greek audience. The best way to reconcile these two stories is to see them as reports of the same event provided to different groups.

In the account of Jesus' feeding five thousand men, we see parallel events meshing into one large theological sequence. Earlier in chapter 6 Jesus sent the disciples on a ministry field trip (6:6b-13). He had equipped and empowered them to preach a call to repentance and to work miracles. Despite still being in the formative stage and not yet fully seeing Jesus as being both Messiah and God, their mission had been deemed successful. It was upon their return that Jesus wanted to move away from the crowds and find a quiet place to rest and debrief. As Scripture explains, Jesus was routinely attracting crowds and found it all but impossible to find solitude: "So they went away by themselves in a boat to a solitary place. But many who saw them leaving recognized them and ran on foot from all the towns and got there ahead of them" (6:32-33).

Jesus lived as a curious celebrity during this part of his life. Many were drawn to him as the actual Messiah; their allegiance to him was spiritual and based on faith. Others were excited by his teachings and his supernatural abilities, though they didn't see him as anything more than a gifted rabbi. To the religious rulers, Jesus was an aberration, a heretic, and a deluded rube from Nazareth who dared suggest that God had sent him to redeem the world. Each of these groups, along with those who had yet to register an opinion of Jesus, made up the crowd of nearly twelve thousand that confronted him upon his arrival. *Will he teach us? Will he do any tricks?*

As Thomas Oden writes, "Jesus did not come to deliver a gospel, but to be himself that gospel" (11). This gospel was central to all that Jesus taught, especially when the needs of the people were so evident. This had to have been the case as he looked out onto the assembling crowd: "When Jesus landed and saw a large crowd, he had compassion on them, because they were like sheep without a shepherd. So he began teaching them many things" (v. 34). Scripture doesn't record the mindset of the disciples upon seeing the crowd, but it's likely that they were not pleased. These spiritually immature men were exhausted from their mission trips, yet they were eager to brag to Jesus about all they'd experienced. This was supposed to be a guys' weekend with the Boss, not another crusade event. Jesus, on the other hand, was moved to compassion by the sight of the aimless, endangered mass of humanity. R. C. H. Lenski writes,

> In spite of all the unbelief that Jesus encountered, and in spite of His desire to withdraw from His great public activity and to be alone with His disciples, His heart was moved at the sight of all the crowd that had so rapidly and eagerly followed Him. . . . The eyes of Jesus saw more than a mass of people, they saw the spiritual condition of those people. He saw the fate of these people unless they were shepherded. (262–63)

The verb phrase "felt compassion" is used only in reference to Jesus in the New Testament and has a much deeper meaning than any routine human emotion. James McGowan states, "In the Synoptic Gospels it is used with a theological meaning expressing the divine mercy present within Jesus" (87). The *Theological Dictionary of the New Testament* defines the verb as "a Messianic characterization of Jesus rather than the mere description of an emotion" (Kittel and Friedrich, 554).

It is difficult for today's reader to understand the plight of the Jews during the time of Jesus. Many had grown cold in their faith and lived merely as cultural Jews. Spirituality played little to no part in their daily lives. High and holy days came and went with ceremony but without passion. Faith practices were rote and meaningless. Their spiritual leaders were hard-hearted and cold. A segment of the leadership wanted to overthrow Rome to establish a church-state. Another group wanted to keep peace with the occupiers in order to remain in quasi-power and position. All in all, the Jews had no vision and no leadership. As a people they were going nowhere. Jesus acted to give them a renewed vision and a path back to God's will and purpose. This was indeed a dangerous time for Israel:

Israel is here portrayed as a people without direction, purpose, or leadership. They, like sheep, were helpless, exposed and lost. This prompted within Jesus a desire to 'teach them many things.' It is interesting to note that Jesus' compassion is expressed first and foremost in that He saw their need for sound doctrine and supplied it. (McGowan, 86–87)

The Hebrew religious leaders had perverted sound theology and doctrine, choosing to create a curriculum that met their needs rather than the needs of the nation as a whole. This break with priestly responsibility left the Jews exposed to the elements of a world spinning away from the one true God. A sad diffusion of roles had taken place within Judaism. The people group chosen to lead the world to God were now lost, aimless, and in need of a path to God. Jesus knew this as he looked upon the crowd. He took redemptive pity and expressed his power to provide them opportunity to return home.

The New Communion

Jesus took time to teach the crowd "many things," likely spending much of the afternoon before them. Scripture indicates that it was "late in the day" when the disciples approached Jesus and suggested that he send the large crowd on their way so they could find places to purchase food. Jews traditionally traveled with a food basket filled with ceremonially clean food to ensure that no dietary laws would be broken while they were away from home. The fact that so many people were without food so late in the afternoon suggests they left home unprepared and in a hurry to see Jesus, or that they had already consumed the food they brought with them. Most likely they had already eaten their food due to the unanticipated length of time they shared with Jesus. Either way, the people were far from home and hungry, and the night would soon be upon them. Mark cites "green grass" (v. 39), making this late spring when sunset occurred no later than 6:00 in the evening. All of this tells us that there was little remaining time for this mass of people to find their own provisions.

It is hard to determine the disciples' motivations in wanting Jesus to dismiss the large crowd. David Garland suggests they may have been motivated by an altruistic concern for the people or by a selfish desire for privacy so that they could at last eat in peace (253). Jesus didn't ponder the request of the disciples; he simply told them to give the people "something to eat" (v. 37). It would be fascinating to know what the disciples were thinking at that moment. *What? Us? With what exactly are we to feed five thousand men, plus their wives and children? We are hungry, too, you know.* Any altruistic motives might have evaporated at this point: "They said to him, 'That would take eight months of a man's wages! Are we to go and spend that much on bread and give it to them to eat?'" (v. 37).

One of the disciples was good at math and quickly estimated that Jesus' request would cost a fortune *if* (and it would have been a big "if") they possessed that much money and *if* there was that much food available to be purchased in such a remote area. Add that it was nearing dusk, and the difficulties were compounding as they spoke. The *Life Application Bible Commentary* describes the disciples' plight this way: "The disciples summed up the situation and found it hopeless" (Barton et al., 179). This situation is reminiscent of Moses' experience in Numbers 11 as Israel had grown tired of manna and wanted meat (Num 11:13). God has a tendency to provide in unorthodox ways, but then again, aren't miracles unorthodox by their nature? God responded to Moses, "Is the LORD's power limited?" Jesus took a different tack: "How many loaves do you have? Go and see."

Since the disciples continued to operate with an amazing lack of faith and were already quite skilled at missing the point, Jesus took it easy on them. Their on-the-job training was progressing slowly, and this was a true teachable moment. He simply responded with, "Well, what do you have?" They looked around and reported that five loaves of barley bread and two dried fish were all they had. To the disciples it was just enough food for one hungry man. To Jesus it was the basic ingredients for a major miracle. He told the disciples to arrange the people in groups of 100 and 50. Why such a neat arrangement? No one really knows why, but it has been suggested that it was done to emulate further what Moses did with Israel (Exod 18:21). It is also likely that the men were separated from the women and children as was the Hebrew custom. The disciples stopped asking questions and simply did as Jesus instructed. It was time for the Shepherd to feed his sheep.

Once the people were arranged, Jesus took the five loaves and two fish, looked up to heaven, sought God's blessings on the unique communion meal, and then broke the bread. The miracle occurred as Jesus broke the bread. The verbs in this verse are in different tenses in the original language. "Broke" signifies the instantaneous and "gave" implies a continuous act. Jesus broke the bread and continued to give bread to the disciples until five thousand men were fed. The miracle grows larger when all of the people are accounted for as the actual number likely exceeded twelve thousand. The disciples became servers and fed the people until all were satisfied: "So they all ate and were filled" (v. 42).

Mark doesn't provide insight into the crowd's reaction to this miracle but John's version does: "Then those men, when they had seen the sign (miracle) that Jesus did, said, 'This is truly the Prophet who has come into the world'" (John 6:14).

Life Lessons

Scholars have long debated the significance of this miracle sequence and sought to mine every ounce of theological meaning from it. Those who seek to minimize the miracles of Jesus have deduced that Jesus had a large amount of food hidden away and the miracle feeding was a ruse. One would have to strive mightily to make this lame attempt of discrediting Jesus stand to all scrutiny. Jesus would have needed a silo filled with food to pull that off, and his sleight of hand would have been worthy of a Las Vegas headliner. *Now Appearing Nightly . . . !* Others have linked this miracle to the act of communion, although there was no fish at the Last Supper and only one loaf of bread. While this wasn't prescient of a Eucharist meal, it does have larger communion overtones. Jesus broke the bread and fed people until the need for food abated. He looked to heaven for the blessings of God. Days later Jesus would again look to heaven to seek God; then he would die of a broken body. "This is my body which is broken for you."

Two thousand years after this event, the church still seeks the nourishment only Christ can deliver. It should be our daily mandate to seek the wisdom of God through Scripture, worship, and prayer. It is by these means that we are fed. It is by being fed that we are able to grow and develop and become the people of God. We must also take on a dependent spirit and never lose sight of our need for God's care. Muslims are required to pray five times per day so that they will not forget Allah. Christians should pray, attend to Scripture, worship, and serve God daily as a way to demonstrate that we not only remember God, but also that we utterly depend upon God to meet basic needs. *Bread of Heaven, feed me 'til I want no more* must be our daily mantra.

Jesus must also be seen as our personal Shepherd. We too can drift far from home and lose sight of the grassy meadows where we are protected and cared for. Just as Israel had become divided and carnal, or as McGowan puts it, "people without direction, purpose or leadership" (86), we too need the steady hand of our Shepherd. It has been said that the only sheep needing a shepherd are those who graze where there is no fence. Life is lived in a world without fences. God provides for our spiritual existence. We can be people with direction, purpose, and leadership. All it takes is five loaves of barley bread, two small fish, and God.

1. Discuss reasons Jesus drew such large crowds wherever he went.

_____

_____

_____

_____

_____

_____

2. In what ways might modern readers _undervalue_ this miracle sequence?

_____

_____

_____

_____

_____

_____

3. Cite similarities between the miracle feeding of the wandering Israelites and the feeding of the five thousand.

_____

_____

_____

_____

_____

_____

4. Contrast the reactions of Jesus and the disciples to this great need.

_____
_____
_____
_____
_____
_____

5. Is there theological significance in the incredible monetary amount the disciples guessed it would take the buy food for the multitude? Cite examples.

_____
_____
_____
_____
_____
_____

6. How have skeptics reasoned away this miracle to discredit Jesus as miracle worker?

_____
_____
_____
_____
_____
_____

7. Is there theological significance in Jesus arranging the multitude in twelve rows and on the "green" grass? Explain.

_____
_____
_____
_____
_____
_____

8. Thomas Oden wrote, "Jesus did not come to deliver a gospel, but to be that gospel" (11). What can the modern believer learn from this statement?

_____

_____

_____

_____

_____

_____

6

Jesus on Divorce

Mark 10:1-9

Jesus was an itinerant rabbi who drew crowds: "A large crowd gathered around him and once more, as his custom was, he taught them" (Mark 10:1b). This portion of Mark's account describes a geographical shift in Jesus' movement as he traveled from Galilee to Judea. This would place Jesus on a collision course with Jerusalem and a final confrontation with the Pharisees. The Hebrew religious leaders had determined that the only way to deal with Jesus was to kill him (in the name of God, of course). Jesus had already spoken of this inevitability twice, but the disciples continued to be oblivious to his prophetic words.

Jesus and his disciples traveled south along the Jordan River through the Samaria region and stopped in Judea where John the Baptist had earlier preached. Jesus was already well known in this area and quickly drew large crowds to hear his prophetic pronouncements. Among the throng were local Pharisees, who came up with a plan to trap Jesus by asking specific questions about divorce. Divorce has been a part of all social and cultural fabrics for almost as long as the institution of marriage has been in place. God ordained marriage between a man and a woman as part of the creation order, and it is common for Christians to view marriage as being both holy and intrinsically linked with God's larger relationship with humankind. Marriage is foundational to God's overall equation for the created order. The *created order*, however, had responsibilities to treat marriage as a uniquely high and holy institution.

Over time marriage became primarily a social institution that fell prey to the self-absorption that divides the spiritual "ideal" from the spiritual "real." Beginning with Lamech's initiation of bigamy (*polygamy* is having multiple spouses; *polygeny* is having multiple wives), marriage became devalued. Lamech was a descendant of Cain and was not known for his spiritual devotion to God. His pronounced drift from traditional marriage influenced many future leaders of Israel such as Jacob, Saul, David, and Solomon.

Today's society is also marked by fractious views of what constitutes a "proper" marriage. It is possible in some states to marry within one's own gender. Divorce as a rule is easy and relatively cheap to obtain in all fifty states. The Census Bureau data states that between 1970 and 1996, the number of divorced people in the United States increased from 4.3 to 18.3 million people (Saluter and Lugaila, 1). The decade of the 1970s is known as the high water mark for divorces in the U.S., with the rate more than doubling from 2.5 to 4.8 per 1000 population between 1965 and 1975 ("Monthly Vital Statistics Report," 7). In the twenty-first century, it is commonly believed that half of all marriages end in divorce. This isn't necessarily true as national data reports that rates of divorce have steadily declined since 1981, settling at 3.6 divorces per 1000 people in the twelve months prior to September 2006 (Lopatto). This would mean that the overall divorce rate in America has declined by 1.5 percentage points since 1980. That's the good news; the bad news is the number of people getting married has steadily decreased. This reality causes more than a bit of blurring of the data and tends to dull the positive impact of fewer divorces.

The General Social Survey provided specific social data on marital outcomes by religion in the United States (Wright). For evangelical Christians who self-reported church attendance of at least once per week, the divorce rate was 34 percent. A separate category listed mainline Protestant Christians who reported the same attendance practices with a 32 percent rate of divorce. In contrast, both non-active mainline Protestants' and evangelicals' rate of divorce was 42 percent. The catch-all non-Christian group had a 48 percent rate. Jews were not asked about synagogue attendance practices and demonstrated a divorce rate of 39 percent. The bright spot among all religions was Catholicism with a divorce rate of only 23 percent among those who considered themselves active. The American Muslim community is also seeing an increase of divorce among adherents living in the United States. Historically Islam has allowed for male-dominated divorces and for up to four wives per man. In the West, however, Islam has lived within the statutes of national, regional, and state regulations. Divorce has not been an overly active part of the Western Muslim experience until recently:

> Divorce is on the rise in the Muslim community, especially in the West. According to a study conducted by Dr. Ilyas Ba-Yunus, a sociology professor at State University of New York, the overall divorce rate among Muslims in North America is at an astounding 31 percent. The state of California ranks highest with a 37 percent rate and New York, Ontario and Texas follow closely with a 30 percent rate. Compared to the overall divorce rate in the U.S. and Canada, the increasing rate of divorce among Muslims is cause for alarm. (Kholoki)

The U.S. Census Bureau also reports that marriages between Baby Boomers born at the peak of that generation (1945–54) last longer than those between younger Americans. Of first marriages for women born between 1945 and 1954, 79 percent marked their fifteenth anniversary, compared with only 57 percent of those who married for the first time from 1985 to 1989. Other notable information from the 2004 Marriage and Divorce Census Bureau document includes the following:

- On average, first marriages that end in divorce last about eight years.
- The median time between divorce and a second marriage was about three and a half years.
- In 2004, 12 percent of men and 13 percent of women had married twice, and 3 percent each had married three or more times.
- Among adults 25 and older who had ever divorced, 52 percent of men and 44 percent of women were currently married.
- Just over half of currently married women in 2004 had been married for at least 15 years, and 6 percent had been married at least 50 years. (U.S. Census Bureau)

In a society that has lowered its divorce rate by inventing the prenuptial agreement, marriage is obviously moving away from God's ideal. It would be an insult to the first-century Jews to suggest they were abusing divorce in manners worse than today's flawed societal practices. This is why the discussion between Jesus and the Pharisees remains the pivotal teaching on divorce in the New Testament. While one could argue that his words were rigid and impossibly difficult, it is the context of Jesus' pronouncements that provide the key for faithfully aligning with God's perfect plans for humankind.

The Pharisees approached Jesus as he was speaking to the crowd that had quickly gathered upon his arrival into new territory. This was obviously a trap arranged by the religious leaders who wanted to damage Jesus in the eyes of the masses and have ample witnesses in case Jesus spoke out against Herod. Divorce was both a dangerous and fractious topic for the Jews at that point, especially following Herod's marriage to his brother's former wife. The Pharisees would have seen this as the perfect way to expose Jesus as an imposter messiah and to elevate their already cozy relationship with Herod. Jesus, however, did not fall prey to their attack; in short order he placed much of the blame for selfish divorces with them.

> Some Pharisees tested him by asking, "Is it lawful for a man to divorce his wife?"
>
> "What did Moses command you?" Jesus replied.
>
> They said, "Moses permitted a man to write a certificate of divorce and send her away."
>
> "It was because your hearts were hard that Moses wrote you this law," Jesus replied. "But at the beginning of creation God 'made them male and female.' For this reason a man will leave his father and mother and be united to his wife, and the two will become one flesh. So they are no longer two, but one. Therefore what God has joined together, let man not separate." (Mark 10:2-9, author's paraphrase)

Issues relating to marriage and divorce were not new to Judaism, as Moses was forced to make allowances for divorce among the wandering Israelites hundreds of years before Jesus. As the various schools of theological thought formed, one of the most striking differences was centered on divorce. Lamar Williamson Jr. writes, "The question about divorce was a burning one among the Pharisees just after and perhaps during Jesus' time, for the Talmud reports arguments about legal grounds for divorce among various authorities within the Pharisaic movement (Shammai, Hillel, Aqiba)" (175). Add Herod's questionable marital practices to this convoluted mix, and the Pharisees' question to Jesus becomes the quintessential "lose-lose" situation. The question was framed in such a way that it couldn't be answered without breaking with Herod, the titular head of Israel, or with one of the orthodox schools of theology within Judaism. The authors of *Matthew and*

Mark: Good News for Everyone illuminate the impossibility of answering this question:

> To better understand the tests the Pharisees were giving Jesus, it helps to know that his peers would have been exposed to the teachings of Rabbi Hillel and Rabbi Shammai, two noted scholars born a generation or so before Christ. Both had great wisdom but they disagreed on a great many topics. For example, after both Rabbis had studied Deuteronomy 24:1, the conservative school of Shammai ruled that "something about her that he doesn't like" meant adultery. The liberal school of Hillel, however, claimed that a man could divorce his wife for *anything* that displeased him, even burning a meal. If Jesus had sided with either of these men's teachings on divorce, he might well have lost the following of all those who supported the other. (Leston and Strauss, 180)

Jesus opted to respond to their question with a question of his own: "What did Moses command you?" This had to have irritated the Pharisees, who were accustomed to being able to control others through their position and power. It is surprising that Scripture doesn't record one of them shouting, "Just answer the question!" Unwittingly the Pharisees switched places with Jesus and became the prey rather than the hunter. Jesus led them to make his point about divorce; that divorce was permitted due to the sorry spiritual state of Israel. By admitting "Moses permitted a man to write a certificate of divorce and send her away," they gave Jesus opportunity to move beyond both theological schools and to reestablish God's original intentions for marriage.

The Pharisees answered with what Moses *permitted*, but Jesus spoke of what God *commanded*. The difference between the two stances is neither nuanced nor petty. It is the equivalent difference between day and night. David Garland writes, "This response opens the door for Jesus to make his point: Divorce is not a command but a concession because of hardness of heart. The legal stipulations do not mean that God approves of divorce" (60–61). Jesus' response seemed to confuse the Pharisees and was counterintuitive to current Hebrew practice. It was as if they had become oblivious to God's earliest commands for marriage. The *Life Applicaton Bible Commentary* continues,

The Pharisees thought Jesus was referring to Moses' writing in Deuteronomy 24:1-4; but Jesus' response reveals that he was referring to Moses' words in Genesis about the ideal state of creation and particularly of marriage. Moses did not command divorce; instead he recognized its presence, permitted it, and gave instructions on how it should be carried out. (Barton et al., 280)

In Deuteronomy, Moses was responding to the growing reality of divorce within Judaism. It obviously wasn't what God ordained through creation, but it was the current state of God's people. Truth be told, Israel was not living out their calling to be a nation of priests and a holy nation. Rather than salting the earth with their difference, they had become eerily similar to all other groups. History shows that Israel consistently moved away from God, and in so doing became closer to their pagan neighbors than to God's ideal. Multiple, fast, and frivolous divorces were evidence of their backsliding and the ever-shifting laws adopted to justify their behavior. This is one of the reasons Jesus stated that he "had not come to destroy the law, but to fulfill it" (Matt 5:17).

Embedded in Jesus' words is evidence of the coming reality of life under a new type of law. The new law would be written on the hearts and souls of his people and not on parchment and stone. The new law would be fluid and based in the Spirit of God. In an odd way, Jesus was telling them that the new law would effectively put them out of business. It had taken their kind several centuries to obfuscate the original tenets of Hebrew law and turn it into a tedious, voluminous, and restrictive form. They would send their wives away for burning toast but would not get an ox out of a ditch on the Sabbath. Somehow they had become blind to the utter ridiculousness of what they had created. A sick person could not get better through treatment on the Sabbath, but old Jewish guys were trading in their wives for newer models. As Jesus said, their hearts were hardened to it all.

The temptation at this point is to beat up on the spiritually deaf and blind Pharisees and miss an important point: What does Jesus' response to the Pharisees mean to today's church? The answer is short and simple: Divorce remains outside of God's will for his people. Nothing has changed theologically in the intervening two thousand years. Yet, the people of God continue to divorce their spouses, often for insubstantial reasons. This is proof that Jesus' words reaffirming the centrality of marriage to God's overall plans for creation remain necessary for the modern church. Mark's rendering of Jesus and the Pharisees continues to provide a sound theological framework for the church. While the ironclad teaching seems harsh and unyielding, it is an accurate portrayal of God's will. It does not, however, deal with extenuating circumstances that lead to many justifiable divorces. Jesus does not deal with issues of abuse or abandonment that leave the spouse with little choice other than divorce. Contextually, his teaching was absolute due to the spiritual laxity and selfish attitudes of the Hebrews, especially among their supposed spiritual leaders.

Life Lessons

A key teaching in the New Testament focuses on a selfless devotion to God. This life of denying our innate carnal instincts will bring us closer to God and God's will for our lives. This same selfless spirit must also be applied to marriage. God chose to weave marriage into the creation tapestry, and we must not lose sight of its primacy in God's order. As David Garland writes, "Divorce is sin in God's eyes because it originates in human hardness of heart" (380). Divorce also brings with it both real and collateral damage. Judy Bodmer states,

> If you divorce your spouse at first, you might find relief, but that is short-lived. Tests show that for the first five to six years, you will be consumed by moderate to severe anger. Depression, which at its very core is a feeling of failure, will become your companion. Stress tests rank separation and divorce as the second and third most traumatic events in a person's life. This shouldn't be surprising when you look at the Bible. The word used for (they shall become one) "flesh" is the same word used to describe the attachment of muscle to bone. The pain of tearing living tissue is the pain of tearing apart a relationship. (8)

Divorce does holistic damage and is prone to take prisoners. However, divorce isn't always equal opportunity in its distribution of damage. One who instigates a divorce may be seeking "to find themselves," or determine that "they really were not in love with their spouse." These justifications rank with the Hebrew "burning of toast" in violating God's intentions for marriage. Jesus was reacting against the easy, selfish, and frivolous divorces that devalued both marriage and God's plans for humankind. If the marital relationship is to mirror the individual's spiritual union with God, then a selfish dissolution of marriage would be completely counter to God's will. This is the primary reason that divorce is considered a sin. That said, however, what about the innocent partner in a dissolved marriage? Is he or she living in sin?

Theologically speaking the answer would be *yes*—even the innocent partner has sinned as *any* divorce is seen as counter to God's will. Please do not see this sin as being unpardonable, however, as theologically a sin is a sin is a sin. The sin of divorce is one that God forgives just as God forgives the many other sins we commit in the daily course of life. The old saying is trite but true: God hates the sin but loves the sinner. Jesus proved many times over that he came to rectify our sin conditions, including divorce. The key is not to abuse the legal provisions for divorce for personal gain as did the Hebrews. Jesus condemned divorces for personal gain or selfish indulgence. He reacted against the proclivity of trading in an old spouse for a newer, flashier model. This practice would suggest that it's all about us. It isn't. It's all about God!

1. Why were the Pharisees hoping to trap Jesus with their questions?

_____

_____

_____

_____

_____

_____

2. Describe the lax morals and standards concerning marriage and divorce that Jesus spoke out against.

_____

_____

_____

_____

_____

_____

3. Discuss the idea of the spiritual "real" versus the spiritual "ideal" as it pertains to marriage and divorce.

_____
_____
_____
_____
_____
_____

4. Discuss reasons U.S. divorce rates are higher within the Christian community than in the general population.

_____
_____
_____
_____
_____
_____

5. Moses permitted divorce in order to gain some level of control over the growing practice. What should be done today to lessen the number of divorces?

_____
_____
_____
_____
_____
_____

6. Is it always a sin to divorce one's spouse?

_____
_____
_____
_____
_____
_____

7. What are *justifiable* reasons for divorce?

_____

_____

_____

_____

_____

_____

8. Understanding Jesus' teaching on divorce, what would be *unjustifiable* reasons for divorce?

_____

_____

_____

_____

_____

_____

9. How do you relate Jesus' repeated use of "hardness of heart" to today's society and church in regard to marriage?

_____

_____

_____

_____

_____

_____

10. Summarize God's will for marriage.

_____

_____

_____

_____

_____

_____

Jesus and the Rich Young Ruler

The world of Jesus was getting smaller as he made his way toward Jerusalem and his fate on the cross. He was becoming more popular with the people and subsequently less so among the religious leaders. His teaching was charged with cutting-edge pronouncements that would in time lead to seismic shifts in both culture and religion. As he moved toward his date with crucifixion, he lived and spoke a theology that would define a new movement. Mark has Jesus responding to the Pharisees on divorce, chastising his disciples for turning away eager children, and being stopped in his tracks by a wealthy man who wanted advice on salvation. All of this took place in an unnamed town over the course of a few days. All of these events in their own unique and disparate ways helped frame the foundation of our doctrine and theology. The modern church owes a great deal to Jesus' time in a village so insignificant that it was not even named.

After jousting with the devious Pharisees about divorce and the sadly clueless disciples about the special place of children, Jesus is attempting to leave town when he is stopped by a young man inquiring about salvation. The ensuing conversation is fascinating because this person of privilege asks a question that the Pharisees already should have asked Jesus. Of course, the Pharisees assumed they already knew all the answers, for they had a rulebook. This is also the only instance recorded in Mark's account of a rich person asking questions of Jesus. Plus, when combining this event with the previous account of Jesus' blessing the children, a strong theological case for Christian atonement emerges. The *Life Application Bible Commentary* states,

This episode with the rich young man contrasts sharply with the previous episode of Jesus blessing the children. The children are an example of faith and trust; they do nothing to gain eternal life, but they receive it because of their simple faith. The rich young man thought he could gain eternal life by what he did, only to find that he could not have it. (Barton et al., 288)

This young man asked a question that is foundational to our theology and doctrine as Christians: "What must I do to inherit eternal life?" (10:17). He, like the vast majority of Jews, saw eternal life as a state to be achieved. A person *did* certain things in order to merit salvation. This would have been true throughout all social strata within Judaism. Earned salvation was part and parcel to the Mosaic Law and was grounded in the original commandments. Being wealthy and privileged may have previously shielded the young man from the full impact of Jesus' gospel. R. Alan Cole writes, "He probably belonged to a social group as yet scarcely touched by the gospel . . . " (232).

Whether he was already familiar with Jesus is unknown; nonetheless, he ran to catch up with Jesus as he was walking away from the village with his disciples. He was eager and honest in his solicitation of Jesus, which would have placed him on a different plane of intent from the Sadducees and Pharisees. Jesus stopped to deal with the young man, although he may not have had a choice because the kneeling questioner blocked his path. McGowan sums up the importance of this encounter:

> The first thing that stands out in this verse is the fact that this man came with a sense of urgency. He ran to Jesus, kneeled, and addressed him formally, suggesting respect and sincerity of heart. This question must have pleased Jesus because, up to this point in time, no one had asked such a profound question, not even Jesus' own disciples. This was *the* question that everyone should have been asking. (141)

In the process of first addressing Jesus, the young man referred to him as "Good Teacher" (v. 17). *Good* as an adjective was used almost exclusively by the Jews to refer to God. It would have been the rarest of rabbis who were called "good," so either the young man sensed that Jesus was spiritually special or he was "buttering up" Jesus as the saying goes. Scholars are divided on the man's rationale for using this unique term. Some see an almost evil intent in his address while others believe he was simply being humorous. There are others who believe the young man was being sincere but overly emotional. William Barclay follows this line of thinking as he suggests what Jesus may have meant: "No flattery! Don't call me good! Keep that word for God! It looks almost as if Jesus was trying to pour cold water on that young enthusiasm" (*The Gospel of Mark*, 283). In light of the magnitude of the question, it is unlikely that Jesus was being obstinate; he was never recorded as being cruel to those seeking him. For some unknown reason, Jesus neither denied nor promoted his Deity, rather he gently corrected the young man and answered his question. It was, however, not the answer the man was hoping to hear.

As it turns out, this man was in the right place at just the right time. Not only was Jesus passing through his area, but he was also in the process of redefining salvation through his teaching and life examples. Jesus was in the process of literally altering the structure of salvation by elevating it exclusively to the level of a grace gift. This new rendering of salvation was difficult for the Jews to understand because it conflicted with the traditional views of the Mosaic Law. Israel's theology of salvation was rooted in Israel's covenant relationship with God. A. J. Conyers sums up the traditional Hebrew views of salvation this way:

> [T]he impulse to do what is right and to require what is right in both individuals and the community, was not something other than religion; it was the very heart of religion. That human beings desire to do what is right and resist wrong is relevant to the worship of God. If God has placed within us the desire for good, and instructed us with a revealed Law, supporting the good and punishing the evil, then that righteousness or justice (i.e., the right and just way) must be the very nature of God. (160)

This eager and good young man was being very Hebrew in seeing the law as written in stone. Yes, righteousness and justice previously had been given to those who honored God by word, deed, and adherence to the Law. To him the Law was a "thing" and certainly not a person, and certainly not the person standing before him. "The very nature of God" was answering his question! Sadly, though, the young man could not make the leap beyond the jot and tittle of the Law. Of course, it could have been Jesus' difficult and unique requirement that led the man away. If someone came up to you on the street and asked you what they needed to do to inherit eternal life, you would tell them to believe in Jesus as savior and confess all their sins. You might even offer to pray with them to assist with their conversion and commitment. It stands to reason that you wouldn't tell them to go sell all their earthly possessions and contribute their earnings to the poor. If that were the entry fee, heaven would be a lonely place for sure. And think how many fewer churches we would need. I'm guessing twelve or thirteen would suffice for the entire country.

The Hebrew Way

The Old Testament states that righteousness was imputed to Abraham for his willingness to sacrifice Isaac. Micah wrote the quintessential verses on Hebrew righteousness: "He has told you what is good; and what does the Lord require of you but to do justice, and to love kindness, and to walk humbly with your God" (v. 8). In each case the primary focus is in the verb form and signifies an act. Judaism was founded on the platform of monotheism and right actions. As a "nation of priests and a holy nation," Israel was to demonstrate detailed devotion to the Most High God in order to influence and lead other people groups into a reconciled relationship with God. They would accomplish their calling by living righteously and justly and by following the basic tenets of the Law. Over time, however, their works-based faith structure devolved into a "means to an end" approach to religion. The essence behind their actions slowly faded into a rote practice of legalism. The relational aspects gave way to hard-line attention to rules and sub-rules. The Sabbath became more of a day not to do things than a day of worship and celebration.

Sadly, Judaism in the early first century was at its rote worst in terms of a relation-less approach to legalistic religion. Without fully realizing it, the Hebrews had raised the bar on achieving salvation to all but unreachable heights. Judaism promoted a hollow emptiness that permeated Hebrew society and made it easier for the religious elite to oppose Jesus. The Spirit had been *ruled* out.

The Christian Way

Jesus ushered in a new era for humankind's salvation based on faith rather than actions. It is all but impossible to overstate the differences between the evolved salvation requirements of the Hebrews and those espoused by Jesus. Setting a record for consecutive days without breaking a commandment would no longer qualify a person for eternal life. Eternal life, or salvation, would come through belief and faith in Jesus as redeemer. Jesus effectively lowered the bar for salvation and, in the process, opened God's love for all people. Jesus' offer of salvation was "equal opportunity" where Israel's Law was discriminatory. Jesus was clear, however, that he had not come to destroy the law; rather, he had come to embody and perfect it (Matt 5:17). The Hebrew Law became perfect in Jesus.

Say What?

It is unlikely that this wealthy young man knew he was conversing with God, despite his use of "Good Teacher" in addressing Jesus. As we noted in the previous session, "good" was used almost exclusively in describing God: "The common Hebrew thought was, 'no one is good but God alone'" (Barton et al., 289). Why Jesus didn't come right out and say to the man, "Who do you think you're talking to, Buster?" is anyone's guess. It seems the perfect opportunity to cement his claim of being the Messiah. Jesus chooses to shift the man's question away from him and onto God. The man asked for an equation for salvation from an esteemed rabbi, but he quickly found himself failing his private tutorial. Was Jesus telling him that no amount of right living can match God's intrinsic goodness and that "qualifying" is no longer an option? In short, yes, but Jesus took the long route and in so doing caused seismic shifts in the minds of both this young man and his disciples.

Jesus was patient and kind in dealing with the man's complicated question: "You know the commandments: Do not commit adultery, do not murder, do not steal, do not bear false witness, do not defraud, honor your father and mother" (10:19). Jesus recited an unordered and slightly different wording of some of the original commandments. Successful stewardship of these particular guidelines would require action, even if that meant "not" doing something (the "shall nots"). He responded to Jesus: "Teacher, I have kept all these since my youth" (v. 20).

His response is remarkable for several reasons. He believed that he had not broken any of these commandments since his thirteenth birthday (when he achieved Hebrew manhood). If his claim is true, and there is no reason to assume it is not, this young man deserves a medal for being a great person. In fact, if salvation was awarded on the basis of meritorious behavior, this guy would be "home free." We are talking about Eagle Scout material, the type of man you hope will marry your daughter. But Jesus was saying that *really* good and *very* consistent were no longer guarantees of eternal life. Salvation would come by faith and would result in good works rather than the other way around.

Jesus' reply to the man is puzzling and must have felt like a dagger to the stomach: "One thing you lack: go, sell everything you have, and give to the poor, and you will have riches in heaven. Then come follow me" (v. 21). This definitely wasn't the answer the wealthy young man was hoping to hear. In fact, this wasn't the answer Jesus gave to anyone else in Scripture. Jesus had encounters with several rich people that led to their salvation by faith alone. Joseph of Arimathea was an elite Jew who professed faith in Jesus as Messiah, and he was not asked to give up his wealth. So why did Jesus ask this one wealthy Hebrew to give up all of his material wealth in order to find salvation?

Some people believe that Jesus was offering this fine young man a spot on the team: "Come follow me." This would have made him the thirteenth disciple, and, just as the original twelve had been asked to do, he would have had to walk away from the trappings of everyday life to follow Jesus. Others believe Jesus was striking a fatal blow against the upside-down theology of Judaism that saw wealth as being an indicator of God's love and blessings. This mindset was prevalent among the Jews and for centuries had been a social divider within Hebrew society. Jesus later speaks to faith difficulties faced by the wealthy due to their assumed personal security: "It is easier for a camel to go through the eye of a needle than for a rich man to enter the kingdom of God" (v. 23). Jesus, however, never condemns wealth in general:

> Many dismiss Jesus' command to sell all and to give it away as totally unreasonable and out of question. Their instinct is right; Jesus does not reject having possessions. Many of his first followers did have possessions. Somebody owned the houses in which he retreated with his disciples. The central issue has to do with one's ultimate loyalty. The point of the story is not to drive home the need for all of Jesus' followers to sell their possessions. Jesus did not insist that Zacchaeus sell all of his goods and give them to the poor. Zacchaeus voluntarily offers to give up half of his possessions and to restore fourfold whatever he may have gained by fraud. Few are willing to divest themselves of whatever provides them security in this life to enter a new quality of life under God's rule. (Garland, 402–403)

The wisdom to be taken from this encounter between Jesus and the rich young man is one of base loyalty. Jesus was not opposed to wealth in general, nor was he calling the man to be the thirteenth disciple. Jesus was exposing the ugly realities of human greed and the resulting barriers to total commitment to God: "Jesus challenged the man to exchange the blessings of this life for those of the life to come" (Bock, 491). This young man could not accept Jesus' path to salvation because the price was too high. His wealth and status defined him. *"Give it all up? Who, me? Are you joking?"* Standing before Jesus and being assured of salvation directly from God did not sway this young man away from his dependence upon his wealth. Devastated, he walked away from Jesus.

The band of twelve watch the episode, and their reaction is worth noting. After the man walked away, Jesus asked them: "How hard is it for the rich to enter the kingdom of God?" (v. 23). Genuine confusion reigned among the disciples, so Jesus asked another question: "Children, how hard is it to enter the kingdom of God? It is easier for a camel to go through the eye of a needle than for a rich man to enter the kingdom of God" (v. 24). Jesus had placed the disciples on a collision course with a radically new chapter of theology: "The disciples were even more amazed, and said to each other, 'Who then can be saved?'" (v. 25). Note that they asked this to each other and not to Jesus. It is likely that they were afraid that his answer would not be one they wished to hear. They, just like the young man, had missed the point entirely. John Killinger writes, "The disciples are amazed, for like most people they take the ownership of property as a sign of God's blessing. But Jesus is undeterred by their attitude, and tries to make them understand. Entering the kingdom is not easy. It requires complete confidence in God. If our dependence is in anything else, we must forsake that" (89).

The exact point of departure from the ancient Hebrew thought to Jesus' radical and startling statement is this: Salvation is possible only through God! This was effectively the end of the works-based salvation theology of the Hebrews. Salvation would be available to all people, and it would come as a grace gift from God. People could not measure the full impact of salvation, nor could they hope to reach a personal state of achieved righteousness. Wealth would no longer be an automatic sign of God's blessings and could be an impediment to fully seeking and accepting Jesus. We all have a "strongest weakness," something that has power or influence over us. The rich young man's "strongest weakness" was his wealth. It was too important for him to give up, even as the ultimate answer to his question. Jesus exposed a truth common to virtually all people: we tend to create many personal gods, but there is room for only one God (Exod 20:3). It is up to us to choose God.

Life Lessons

Jesus came into a world of imperialism and legalistic religion. He brought to this turbulent period an opportunity to experience salvation in new and profound ways. As Messiah, he taught the love of God and the need for repentance. The first-century Hebrew religion would no longer be a morass of legalism and hoops-jumping; instead, it would be about returning God's love and accepting grace as a gift. As Mike Yaconelli states in *Messy Spirituality*, "Spirituality is not a formula; it is not a test. It is a relationship. Spirituality is not about competency; it is about intimacy. Spirituality is not about perfection; it is about connection. Spirituality is not about being fixed; it is about God's being present in the mess of our unfixedness" (13).

The Hebrew leaders had a great many problems with Jesus' radical theology. He seemed to be veering away from a strict adherence to the law and, as a result, was taking salvation from their purview. Being a Pharisee or a Sadducee was a great gig in those days; there was money to be made and people to be led. Plus, the clergy clothes were nice! When the rich young man asked Jesus what he must do to gain eternal life, Jesus asked for blind and full allegiance from the heart. Even though the young man had kept the commandments for many years, his piety and wealth were no longer enough. Jesus commanded him to sell his possessions and distribute the proceeds to the poor; his god of money could no longer hold first place in life. Salvation would be about surrender, but such surrender was too much for him to accept.

We, too, fight Lordship issues and the pull of materialism. We, too, have gods of our own making and choosing; gods who create barriers that rob us of our relationship with *the* God. Only God can fix our unfixedness; we cannot fix ourselves. It is accomplished entirely by grace.

1. Describe the traditional Hebrew teaching on salvation.

_____

_____

_____

_____

_____

_____

2. What were reasons the religious leaders were so vehemently against Jesus?

_____

_____

_____

_____

_____

_____

3. Describe the attributes of the rich young man who confronted Jesus.

_____

_____

_____

_____

_____

_____

4. Was the young man aware of how volatile his question would be? What response did he expect?

_____

_____

_____

_____

_____

_____

Jesus and the Rich Young Ruler

5. How would his great wealth interfere with his hoped-for salvation?

_____

_____

_____

_____

_____

_____

6. Why didn't Jesus require anyone else to "go, sell all of your possessions and distribute the proceeds to the poor, and follow me"?

_____

_____

_____

_____

_____

_____

7. Why were the disciples confused by Jesus' teaching that day?

_____

_____

_____

_____

_____

_____

8. In light of these two distinct views of salvation, how can we best articulate a definition of salvation to today's world?

_____

_____

_____

_____

_____

Jesus on Fig Trees and Temples

Mark 11:11-18

Jesus was in the home stretch of his earthly ministry when he made his unique and triumphal entry into Jerusalem. While his arrival is the stuff of legend, it was not at all what the lead Jews expected of their long-awaited Messiah. Jesus chose to arrive on a borrowed colt, surrounded by hopeful pilgrims singing "Hosanna!" Hosanna literally means "save us now," which was exactly what average Hebrews hoped their Messiah would do with great expediency. Looking back, it is easy to see how Jesus could have been perceived as the "anti-Messiah" by the majority of Jews. His message of repentance and a spiritual kingdom of God was not what the Roman-oppressed Jews wanted to hear. Their ideal Messiah would be of the line of David in more than lineage; they wanted a political and military savior. The relegation of both sin and hard hearts to a new spiritual birth was not on the radar screens of the first century Hebrews. First-century Israel wanted a stone and mortar kingdom, certainly not one with a foundation of repentance and love for all people.

This was the backdrop for Mark's account in chapter 11 of two highly peculiar days in the life of Jesus. Jesus did two un-Jesus-like things during that span that continue to puzzle biblical scholars two thousand years later. He cursed a fig tree for not producing figs even though it was not the season for figs, and he had an angry outburst in the Gentile Court of the temple.

> Jesus entered Jerusalem and went to the Temple. He looked around at everything, but since it was already late, he went out to Bethany with the Twelve. The next day as they were leaving Bethany Jesus was hungry. Seeing in the distance a fig tree in leaf, he went to find out if it had any fruit. When he reached it, he

found nothing but leaves because it was not the season for figs. Then he said to the tree, "May no one ever eat fruit from you again." And his disciples heard him say it. On reaching Jerusalem, Jesus entered the temple area and began driving out those who were buying and selling there. He overturned the tables of the moneychangers and the benches of those selling doves, and would not allow anyone to carry merchandise through the temple courts. And as he taught them he said, "Is it not written: My house will be called a house of prayer for all nations, but you have made it a den of robbers." (Mark 11:11-17)

A common theological doctrine exists concerning Jesus' perfection. Jesus was simultaneously both human and divine, and despite being saddled with being human, he never sinned. Thomas C. Oden cites the early councils and theologians who declared the sinlessness of Jesus: "Church teaching affirms that Christ was conceived, lived, and died without sin and was never unmanageably captive to his passions, although he experienced normal human emotions" (254). Many Christians learned this in summer Bible schools, and while they can't explain it in terms of formal theology, they certainly believe it to be true. So, what should we make of Jesus cursing a helpless fig tree and tossing around tables and chairs in the temple court? If Jesus wasn't mad, then exactly what is required to occur to deem someone mad? If Jesus wasn't angry, what defines genuine anger? If Jesus wasn't acting peculiar, then peculiar people worldwide have lost a seminal event to point to for justification. Let's face it . . . Jesus was flaming angry!

For some reason preachers, teachers, and writers have long held that Jesus did not experience genuine anger. It is as if they cannot bring themselves to admit that anger is anger is anger, and that no amount of parsing of adjectives will alter this fact. It is common to hear that Jesus was *righteously indignant*, but not *angry* or *mad*. With this premise as a foundation, it is easy to harp against human anger while allowing for Jesus to escape scrutiny. Actually, the real reason to cite Jesus' "righteous indignation" is that it allows preachers, teachers, and writers to jump over this section entirely and take the easy road.

Another classic cop-out is to say that Jesus was angry about patently kingdom issues and as such he did not sin. The logical result of this idea is that it is perfectly fine to be angry at things related to God's kingdom. The sticky wicket, however, involves the definition of kingdom *things*. Is world hunger a kingdom issue? How about human trafficking? Ethnic cleansing in the name of God? Anyone gotten really steamed about any of these possibilities lately? A kingdom issue within the modern church might involve the quality of air conditioning or the color of carpet, but not likely something related to a more global nature. If we live in a bubble, we have difficulty seeing beyond the bubble. This was true of the first-century Hebrews, and it remains true today. That said, however, the real question is still, "What was bugging Jesus?"

The key to understanding this section of Mark's account is to admit once and for all that Jesus was indeed angry and that his anger was not sinful. *What?* Take a breath, continue reading, and do not fear that you have just committed the unpardonable sin. To admit that Jesus was angry and that he acted on his anger is to be true to Scripture. If Mark states that Jesus cursed a fig tree and kicked about tables (and likely merchants as well), he did just that. Even John, the writer who focuses more on Jesus' divinity than his humanity, portrays Jesus as being angry. In fact, John is the only chronicler of Jesus who mentions him fashioning a whip to use in clearing the temple. This would make an even stronger case for Jesus' being angry and acting out his emotions on the fig tree and the temple merchants. We need to move beyond the anger questions and focus on why Jesus was moved to display his temper. The integrity of the Gospel accounts is tied to the fig tree and the temple; anger is an ancillary issue. Anger was "minor" to a larger "major," and a key to understanding Christianity is to identify the major. Was Jesus making a theological declaration about less-than-stellar fig production and shoddy temple practices? In a way, yes he was, but his anger had a much larger focal point. Jesus was delivering judgment on Israel in a visual parable with two scenes.

Scene 1: The Fig Tree

Mark writes that on the next day (Monday), Jesus was leaving Bethany to travel back to Jerusalem. Bethany was approximately two miles outside Jerusalem and was where Jesus and the disciples spent their nights during this phase of the ministry journey. Mark also points out that Jesus was hungry, and, after spotting a fig tree in the distance, he went to it hoping to find food. He found it filled with leaves but no fruit. His next words would have both stunned and confused his disciples. He spoke to the tree, "May no one ever eat fruit from you again." But it wasn't fig season! Figs were plentiful in that part of the world; one has to believe that, growing up in the countryside of Nazareth, Jesus would have eaten many figs over the years and would have known they weren't in season. Scottish theologian William Barclay goes as far as saying "the whole story does not seem to fit Jesus at all" (*The Gospel of Mark*, 314). He writes,

> This was the Passover Season, that is, the middle of April. The fig tree in a sheltered spot may bear leaves as early of March, but never did a fig tree bear figs until late May or June. Mark says that it was not the season for figs. Why blast the tree for failing to do what it was not possible for it to do? It was both unreasonable and unjust. What are we to say about it? (314)

The real question must focus on *why* Jesus chose to curse the tree for simply doing what fig trees naturally do. The answer has absolutely nothing to do with figs or fruit. In the first scene of this acted-out parable, Jesus was using the fig tree as a metaphor for Israel:

> Jesus did not curse the fig tree because he was angry at not getting any food from it. Instead this was an acted-out parable intended to teach the disciples. By cursing the fig tree, Jesus was showing his anger at religion without substance. Fruitful in appearance only, Israel was spiritually barren. (Barton et al., 318)

Later Mark records that the following day they returned to the fig tree and found it withered to its roots. Darrell L. Bock writes, "As the fig tree was dead, so was Israel . . . " (500). Jesus was not acting un-Jesus-like after all. This was an episode of God judging Israel for losing its spirituality and its purpose.

Scene 2: The Temple

Next we see Jesus and the disciples arriving at the outer gates of the temple in Jerusalem. The temple in the time of Jesus was worthy of "Wonder of the World" status. Robert H. Stein writes of the temple: "The Temple occupied an area of more than 170,000 square yards. The Temple area was the largest such site in the ancient world" (187). After Herod the Great authorized massive renovation in 20 BC, the temple stood taller and grander than at any time in its history. On this day, however, Jesus was not there to gaze at the gold roof or massive footprint of the temple. This was a day when God visited his temple and found it lacking in every way. Priest-backed merchants were selling sacrificial animals to travelers who had journeyed great distances to celebrate Passover. The priests also required that the annual temple tax be paid in Hebrew currency and offered currency exchange for fees even the Romans would deem exorbitant. David Garland offers this explanation as to how corrupt the Passover commercialization had become:

> The phrase "den of robbers" has influenced the most common view of the causes behind Jesus' action. It assumes that Jesus is protesting because the temple has become a crooked business, defrauding worshipers. The high priestly families did gain wealth from their control of the temple's fiscal affairs, and they were guilty of corruption. Josephus, for example, calls the high priest Ananias the "great procurer of money." Jesus may have objected to the way the financial side of the sacrificial system was run. (435)

It is also easy to assume that Jesus is trying to reform the temple practices and is calling the Hebrew leadership's hand in an attempt to influence reformation. This doesn't, however, square with the larger view of events in play. Jesus began the day as a prophet who cursed a fig tree for not bearing fruit, a metaphor for a spiritually impotent Israel. His anger over the corrupt commercialization of the Court of the Gentiles was that of a reformer; it was the anger of God pronouncing judgment on his people and his temple.

Jesus was angry at the temple leadership also because of their disenfranchisement of Gentile converts. Non-Jews who "converted," or came to faith in the God of the Jews, were not allowed to enter into the innermost courts of the temple. Despite their allegiance to the Most High God, they were treated as second-class believers and as such were restricted to the outer areas of the temple complex. It was in this outer area that the buying and selling of temple merchandise occurred. As a result, the Gentile converts were unable to worship during the Passover season. This obvious and intentional segregation was in conflict with God's earlier pronouncements through the prophets:

> Also the foreigners who join themselves to the LORD,
> To minister to Him, and to love the name of the LORD,

To be his servants, every one who keeps from profaning the Sabbath,
And holds fast my covenant;
Even those I will bring to my holy mountain,
And make them joyful in My house of prayer.
Their burnt offerings and their sacrifices will be acceptable on my altar;
For my house will be called a house of prayer for all the peoples.
(Isa 56:6-7)

Jesus also uses words found in Jeremiah 7:11: "Has this house, which is called by my name, become a den of robbers in your sight? Behold, I, even I, have seen it, declares the LORD" (Jer 7:11). Combined, these Old Testament verses provide the searing indictment against God's people that Jesus delivered. The largest condemnation was directed at the Hebrew leadership who led in the desecration of the temple (for profit, no less) and the absolute segregation against non-Jews and Hebrew women: "The clearing of the temple was a specific reprimand of the chief priests and teachers of the law. It also served to condemn religious exploitation" (McGowan, 159).

These bizarre two days in Jesus' life also provided the religious leaders with another reason to seek to destroy him. He had unflinchingly confronted them, so their next move was to plot to kill him, and they were successful only days later. It's obvious that they were given an opportunity to repent and reform and to lead all of Israel back to God through Jesus. They took the opposite path, however, and chose to remain in power. In time they lost God's provisional blessing, and later, in 70 AD, they lost the temple. Israel defaulted on God's unique calling to be a nation of priests and a holy nation. Insular and elitest, they had broken their covenant relationship with God: "Like tree, like temple; like temple, like nation; the parallel is exact" (Cole, 251). Jesus was not simply angry—he was God bringing judgment.

Life Lessons

There are many things to learn from this unique two-day period in the life of Jesus. Sadly, far too many sermons and lessons have focused on the anger issues and missed the vital messages that lie within the fig tree and temple stories. This is not to suggest that anger is a positive emotion in the life of a believer. Anger is rarely displayed in edifying manners, and as James states, "man's anger does not bring about the righteous life that God desires" (1:20). That said, however, is anger a sin? Should we feel guilty about tendencies toward anger? Is an angry person also a bad person? Andrew D. Lester deals with the questions this way:

> Many Christians have been taught that anger in any shape or form is sinful. This is perhaps the most significant reason you and I feel guilty about anger. Underneath our society's suspicion of anger lies centuries of Christian teaching that anger is evil. Anger has been discounted as part of our "carnal nature" and representative of human depravity. In the Middle Ages anger became identified as one of the seven deadly sins. Fervent sermons have traced anger back to the Fall and suggested that if it were not for original sin, human beings would not be plagued by anger at all. We shall discover (later) that anger originates in creation, not in the fall. We will see that its roots are in our basic humanness rather than our sinfulness. (15)

If it is true that anger comes standard with humanity, then anger is something to be controlled much like other not-so-productive emotions. It is in the Christian's best interests to seek help from God when anger becomes a control problem. Unchecked anger can lead to acts that damage relationships, break laws, and cause stress-related ailments. But Jesus did indeed become angry, and he lashed out at both the tree and those selling sacrificial items and exchanging currency in the temple. Jesus' anger proves that anger in and of itself is not sinful. It is what becomes of the anger that determines sin. Burnt toast and underwear left on the floor are not good reasons for angry outbursts. Petty irritations have nothing to do with God's kingdom. Jesus' anger was *all* about God's kingdom. Jesus was pronouncing judgment upon a spiritually lame and impotent Israel. There is much to be learned from his actions over those two days . . . and little of it pertains to anger.

1. Contrast differences between the Messiah-ship of Jesus and the long-awaited hopes of the Jews.

_____
_____
_____
_____
_____
_____

2. Why did Jesus choose an out-of-season fig tree for a lesson on fruitlessness?

_____
_____
_____
_____
_____
_____

3. Cite ways the church has attempted to temper the reality of Jesus' anger.

_____
_____
_____
_____
_____
_____

4. Why does using the term _righteously indignant_ lessen the impact of these stories?

_____
_____
_____
_____
_____
_____

5. What are the main lessons from the cursing of the fig tree?

_____

_____

_____

_____

_____

_____

6. Why did Jesus react so harshly to the selling of sacrificial items in the Court of the Gentiles?

_____

_____

_____

_____

_____

_____

7. What were the sins of the Hebrew leadership in staging a market in this area of the temple complex?

_____

_____

_____

_____

_____

_____

8. What do you suppose the reactions were among those who witnessed Jesus' outburst?

_____

_____

_____

_____

_____

_____

Jesus on Fig Trees and Temples

9. Why do you suppose the Jews didn't understand the full implications of Jesus' pronouncements?

_____

_____

_____

_____

_____

_____

10. In what ways does judgment pertain to the destruction of the temple some forty years later?

_____

_____

_____

_____

_____

_____

The Might of Mites:
The Widow's Mite
Mark 12:38-44

The 2006 sports film *Invincible* tells the true story of Vince Papale, an out of work Philadelphia school teacher tending bar at night while trying to get back on his feet. Papale was a huge fan of the Philadelphia Eagles football team and a bit of a local legend in one of the area adult football leagues.

The movie focuses on the year 1976, when the Eagles hired new coach Dick Vermeil. Vermeil came to town with the idea of reenergizing the city's passion for the Eagles by holding open tryouts. Thousands of men showed up—among them was Vince Papale. Papale not only impressed the coaches but actually made the team, despite never having played football at any organized level except for a year in high school.

What made the movie special was that all of this happened to Papale while he was going through a particularly difficult divorce. When Papale's wife moved out, she left him with nothing but a letter that simply said, "you'll never go anywhere, never make a name for yourself and never make any money." These words haunted Papale; he couldn't let them go. In fact, in the movie, he carries the letter with him everywhere. Even when he made the Eagles, the viewer gets the sense that more than anything Papale was relieved finally to be able to put his wife's words behind him.

The widow we meet in Mark 12 could be described with these same three sentences. She would never go anywhere, never make a name for herself, and never have any money. Society had reinforced this self-image—she had no standing in the societal hierarchy, no wealth, and no voice in the community. Ironically, in Mark 12, it is this same nameless widow who catches Jesus' attention, earns his respect, and becomes an example for others.

Her significance here in Mark 12 mirrors something we find throughout the biblical narrative. In both the Old and New Testaments, almost any time widows are mentioned generally or specifically, something significant is being conveyed. In both Testaments, how one treats widows is seen as a type of spiritual barometer for the purity of our hearts. It can feel as though the very mention of the term is a biblical caution light signifying that something important is about to happen or to be said.

Widows may have been insignificant in the world when the Scriptures were written, but they never should be mistaken as unimportant in the world the Bible creates. This is certainly the case with the widow we meet in Mark 12. Jesus affirmed her significance, and that reality lives on for all who open themselves to this text. In true gospel fashion, the very "least" in ancient Israel is here rendered as among the most important in the kingdom of God.

The Scribes

Before one delves too deeply into Jesus' encounter with the widow, it is important to backtrack a few steps to verses 38-40 of this same chapter. There the reader finds Jesus speaking about the Jewish scribes. On the periphery, the scribes were everything that the widow was not. They were powerful, educated, devout spiritual leaders who were worthy of respect and attention.

Though the term "scribe" means little to believers today, by the time of Jesus in the New Testament world, these seemingly minor characters had become very significant. In the Old Testament era, scribes were merely record keepers. They kept detailed figures on everything from governmental financial records to information on which duty each particular temple priest had been assigned.

During the days of the exile, scribal responsibilities shifted dramatically, from record keeper to law preserver. They were not merely historians, though. Instead, scribes were seen as primary interpreters and communicators of the Israelite torah to the masses.

By the time of Jesus, they were among the most important of early religious leaders in the temple, similar to Pharisees. If one wanted to know how the law was to be understood and lived, one need look no further than the direction and teachings of the scribes (Mashburn and Collins, 801–802).

In the New Testament world, scribes wore long, flowing robes, had seats of power in the temple, and offered a voice to be heard. In juxtaposing these three verses of criticism of the scribes with the unnamed widow, Mark offers us a glimpse of a revolutionary Jesus who questioned these religious leaders' motivation and behavior. According to Jesus, these scribes might have appeared to be figures to be admired and imitated, but they were, in truth, wolves in sheep's clothing. Sure, they wore fine robes (v. 38), had seats of authority (v. 39), and said long, eloquent prayers (v. 40), but it was all a show. Such rhetoric had no connection to their behavior or to the contents of their hearts.

Jesus points out in verse 40 that the Torah laws—about which the scribes were supposedly experts—explicitly said that widows were to be treated with utmost care, respect, and hospitality. The scribes were taking advantage of widows, seizing their few possessions, and taking their homes.

If *Time* magazine had been published in those days, some scribe would have likely been Person of the Year at one point or another. But Jesus suggested that looks are often deceiving. These scribes were not to be viewed as examples; rather, they were now seen as enemies of God. Their ilk was of little value in God's kingdom.

Before leaving the scribes, it is important to recognize that Jesus' comments in Mark are not meant merely as harsh criticism of these leaders within the Jewish temple hierarchy. Rather, Mark desired for the early church and thus early believers to see themselves within the scribes. Anyone can easily succumb to a faith that is more show than substance. Likewise, making a name for oneself is always a temptation, despite the call of our faith to be focused on making God known (Williamson, 233).

The Widow's Example

Having dropped the bombshell regarding the scribes, Jesus continued the business of turning the tables by focusing on the rich life of this widow whom most everyone else has overlooked. This woman's gift was so small that it would have likely been valued at less than a penny today. Likewise, in a world where one's offering was gauged based on the sound that coins made as they rattled against the inside of the collection box, the widow's mite barely would have been heard. Indeed, one could easily say that the insignificance of her gift was only matched by the insignificance of her personhood in that ancient society.

Thankfully, the resounding echo of her gift rang loudly in the only ears that mattered that day—those of Christ himself. According to Mark, Jesus took note of her and her gift. He recognized her as someone of value and her gift as something of worth. In so doing, he communicated tremendous truth.

In a real sense this narrative questions where one finds value or worth in life. Mark 12 suggests to us that our real identity and worth are wrapped up in God alone. It is as if Christ himself desires to whisper into each of our ears, "in me, you will go somewhere, through me, you can change the world, and because of me, you too can participate in the advancement of the kingdom of God."

This passage also addresses the subject of value as connected not only to the widow, but also to her gift. Though it was a small amount of money, it was of enormous worth in the eyes of Christ. In the economy of God, worth is not based on worldly value. Just as Jesus used five loaves and three fish to feed a hungry crowd and twelve ordinary men to change the world, this text reminds us that God can use anything we offer with our whole hearts to make a difference.

There is a rather poignant tension here as well that may allude to another meaning for this text. With the widow's offering, Jesus seems to be emphasizing that giving a large amount to God *proportionally* is better than giving a large amount *period*. Raymond Brown makes the same assertion when he writes, "to Jesus, sacrifice is measured not by what one gives but by what one has left after giving" (615).

This perspective fits nicely in the gospel world where the idea of tithing is not mentioned by Jesus. This isn't to suggest that Jesus disapproved of tithing; to the contrary, tithing remains a good gauge for faithful giving today. Nonetheless, in the Gospels, Jesus may have been arguing for an even more profound expression. Over and over, Jesus focuses on giving our best rather than upon giving a set amount. If this is correct, our best gifts are much more likely to be a proportion of what we have rather than a set amount that when given may not make a difference in our lives.

One must also recognize in this passage the striking similarity between what the widow does and what Jesus will do at the conclusion of Mark. According to Jesus, this woman gave all she had and this is what pleases God. So too, Jesus will give all—his very life—as the ultimate gift given not *to* God but rather *from* God to all of humanity (Williamson, 234).

One final aspect of this passage is powerful and worth our attention. Verse 44 may appear redundant: " . . . she out of her poverty put in everything she had, all she had to live on." This second phrase, "all she had to live on" may be more accurately translated "her whole life." In other words, the widow's actions as she gave "everything she had" were an outward expression of her spiritual life in which she had already given "her whole life" over to God. Again, the allusions to Jesus' impending death are hard to miss.

In the end, the significance of this passage should be evident in the fact that Mark even spent time with the story. One must remember that Mark is the hasty, not-a-moment-to-spare, nothing-but-the-facts Gospel. All of this only leaves readers to marvel that Mark dwells at all on Jesus' encounter with the widow. Mark may not have preserved her name, but he certainly recognized the power of her life and story!

Life Lessons

The trouble with this passage may be in knowing where to stop rather than where to start when it comes to spiritual applications. There is little doubt why it has remained a favorite text among people of faith throughout the centuries. It is flush with practical, understandable lessons that are applicable to almost every life and season. Let me mention four truths that seem of particular significance.

First, *faith always runs the risk of becoming more about show than substance.* With this passage, it is easy to focus on the widow and her actions while losing sight of the scribes and their behavior. Jesus taught an important lesson by holding the behavior of the scribes in tension with the actions of the widow. They *looked* good on the outside; she *was* good on the inside. In our world, just as in theirs, it is always a temptation for us to focus on excelling in the same outward arena as the scribes rather than investing ourselves fully as did the widow in the matters of the heart.

Second, *the widow reminds us that we are all valuable to the kingdom.* Context is important when it comes to studying this text. If one does not realize how little status widows had in the ancient world, one can easily dismiss one of the messages that Jesus was trying to convey. A basic truth of this narrative is that despite what the ancient world might have thought, this nameless widow was a person of worth. Not only that, but what she had to offer was valuable and significant.

We still live in a world where some individuals and groups are considered without value no matter what they do. Like the widow, they may buy into such an understanding of themselves as well.

Fortunately, the Scriptures remind each of us that our true value and worth are found in nothing other than our identity with God. This is what gives us significance and our lives meaning. It doesn't matter if we are the poorest person or the wealthiest, God and God alone is the source of our identity.

Third, *perhaps the best measure of stewardship is what we have left rather than what we give.* Such a notion offers hope to some and a strong challenge to others. If we are like the widow and have few material things, this is a welcome word as it calls us to focus more on giving sacrificially. If we do have financial resources, though, such a notion can be eye opening. Many of us are able to tithe without the monetary amount affecting our lives or causing sacrifice. We may have met the mandate of giving ten percent, but this may not necessarily be our best. A tithe is a good rule of thumb, but is it the exact posture that God wants us to take?

The difficulty here is that this line of thinking means different things for different folks. If God is more concerned with what we have left over than with what we give, a person who gives three percent of her income to God may please God. At the same time, a person who gives ten percent could be falling far short of God's true expectations for his life. While not an easy concept, such a notion does seem to be more in concert with the themes of the Scriptures than an arbitrary amount that doesn't reflect life situations.

Fourth, *God calls us to give all that we are—not part of what we have.* God is not after a portion of our lives; God is after our full lives. This may be the greatest legacy the unnamed widow leaves us. She was someone who did not seem concerned with her own desires. Rather, she was unquestionably ready and willing to give all that she had and all that she was to God. This was never more evident than in her behavior as we witness it in Mark 12.

1. Describe the lives of widows in the biblical world. How do the Scriptures connect the treatment of widows with an overall assessment of one's spiritual well-being?

_____

_____

_____

_____

_____

_____

2. Have you ever felt like you were a "nobody," that you have accomplished nothing significant with your life? How is that perspective challenged by this passage?

_____

_____

_____

_____

_____

_____

3. What is Jesus' point in comparing the scribes to the widow? In what ways do you see "scribal tendencies" alive and well in the church today?

_____

_____

_____

_____

_____

_____

4. Do you think the widow's gift would be received today in the same way it was received by the temple-goers in this passage from Mark? If so, why do you think many people are able to view the importance of gifts to the kingdom of God only through the lens of their size or value?

_____

_____

_____

_____

_____

The Might of Mites: The Widow's Mite

5. Do you agree with the idea in this session that suggests that God may have higher standards for our giving than simply the idea of a tithe? How do you think such a notion would be received in the church today?

_____

_____

_____

_____

_____

_____

6. Do you struggle with giving all of yourself to God? If so, what area of your life is most difficult for you to hand over to God's control?

_____

_____

_____

_____

_____

_____

7. How difficult is it for you to allow God rather than the world to define your self-worth? Is this a lesson you are passing on to your children or grandchildren?

_____

_____

_____

_____

_____

_____

8. Of all the lessons one can draw from this passage of Scripture, which do you feel is most important? Why?

_____

_____

_____

_____

_____

_____

Excited and Unafraid: The Unexpected Conclusion to the Gospel

Mark 16:1-20

When I was in seminary I served as the minister of a small church in eastern North Carolina. One summer there, I accompanied our youth group to a weeklong church camp on the North Carolina coast. The week was enjoyable for everyone. The worship services and Bible studies were well done, the setting was excellent, and spending time with the students was a genuine treat.

At the conclusion of the week, the staff of the camp invited all of the chaperones to attend an end-of-camp evaluation meeting. As we gathered, everyone was quick to express their overall happiness with everything that had happened. That is, until we got to the evaluation of the worship service. As a part of each worship experience, a drama troupe had provided a skit connected to that evening's theme. While everyone applauded their professionalism and the quality of each performance, there was a great deal of disagreement centered around how each skit resolved itself. Many were concerned that the skits ended with no real sense of what one was to take away from them. This was certainly true, as each performance seemed to conclude abruptly with no real explanation by either the dramatists or anyone else as to what the meaning was.

Others in the meeting had a completely different perspective. They were happy with this aspect of each skit. They applauded the performers for refraining from wrapping each performance up in a neat and tidy way. They felt that it was a good thing that as adults, we were all still disagreeing over what each skit meant. From their perspective, the dramatists had done their job well, for they had sent us out to think further about what we had seen. This would only lead to good conversations with our students, time for critical thinking, and the real possibility that different people could construct different meanings from what had been experienced.

In the end, while it certainly was a lively debate, neither side swayed the other. In fact, our meeting that day ended with the same degree of ambivalence as the skits themselves. What still strikes me about that experience is the way it mirrors our sentiments about the final chapter of Mark, which is at the heart of our session for today. Of all the Gospels, Mark's ending is the most difficult to come to terms with. Rather than resolving the story with resurrection appearances and final commands of a triumphant Jesus, Mark 16:1-8a simply ends with an empty tomb and a trio of women who are both excited and terribly afraid. (I use "8a" in this session to differentiate the earliest version of Mark 16:8 from Mark 16:8 that is known as the shorter ending. That version of Mark 16:8 will be noted as 8b.)

Did Mark mean to end his Gospel this way? Is the fact that this Gospel ending is so different from the others a good thing? If so, what are we to take away from an encounter with this text?

Or is the original ending of Mark a mistake? Should Mark 16:8b-20 be seen as the real conclusion? Did the author originally have a different ending in mind?

Accepting 16:1-8a as the real ending shrouds this text in mystery and leaves us with a number of questions. Including verses 8b-20 allows the Gospel to resolve itself in a much more understandable way. Which is right? What was Mark's intention? What *is* the most appropriate way for this drama to end? These are all seminal questions that must be and will be at the heart of this final session with Mark's remarkable Gospel account.

Which Ending?

While a full quarter of Mark deals with the final week of Jesus' life, this same work dedicates the fewest number of verses to the resurrection of all the Gospels. Over the centuries, scholars have written a great deal trying to unravel the mystery associated with Mark's ending. Understanding the perspectives that have emerged and the theories associated with this chapter requires one to travel down a rather arduous trail that can be rugged, rocky, and tiring. For the purposes of this study, I will summarize the positions without belaboring the issue beyond what is necessary for this session.

First, it is important to recognize that most scholars accept that Mark originally ended with verse 8a because in the two oldest existing manuscripts of the Gospel, this is where the ending occurs. This does not mean, however, that everyone agrees that this is where Mark originally meant to end the book.

While some scholars argue that an open and unresolved ending was Mark's plan and unique contribution, others' ideas are just as plausible. For example, Mark may have either died or been imprisoned before writing his planned conclusion. Or Mark may have written a different ending than what we have, but this part of the manuscript was lost. The rather odd and somewhat confusing way that verse 8a is written lends at least some credence to this idea.

What one should remember is that while scholars differ as to how to explain verse 8a as the ending, they are rather unified in their sense that this *is* where the text did originally end. It may also be helpful to be aware that the idea of Mark ending at verse 8a has existed for hundreds of years. Victor of Antioch is said to have written the first commentary on the book of Mark, and even he ends with verse 8a (Robertson, 129).

Alternate Endings to Mark

So what about verses 8b-20? Why are these verses included in most editions of Mark if they are not likely to be from the hand of the original author of this Gospel? Two suggestions may suffice here. (These two thoughts will be offered while considering the shorter ending of Mark [8b] and the longer ending of Mark [vv. 9-20] together. Considering these two texts together is not meant as a way of overlooking the significant differences that exist between the two but rather as a means of simplification. Further research is certainly encouraged for those who want a deeper understanding of these verses.)

First, while these verses do not appear in the two oldest versions of Mark, they do appear in most other ancient Markan manuscripts. Since their presence is not an isolated incident, we can assume that many in the ancient church found these texts valuable.

Second, even if they are not original to Mark, these passages seem to offer a nice combination of the resurrection appearances that we find in Matthew, Luke, and John. Mark's stories are similar and in no way contradictory to the resurrected Jesus that we meet in the other Gospels. The presence of these verses in Mark allows for the book to end in a way that is thus more in line with its Gospel relatives. While not really adding anything to what we find in

Matthew, Luke, and John, these texts don't call into question anything we find there either.

One must be honest, though, in admitting that this second point is both a blessing and a curse when it comes to the inclusion of these verses in Mark. Since these verses parallel Matthew, Luke, and John so closely, many scholars assume that the author of this text was familiar with the other Gospels. Rather than Matthew and Luke borrowing from the older Gospel Mark, as is generally the case, here it appears that the opposite is happening. While the similarity of these verses to Mark's Gospel cousins makes them worth including, it also further convinces most experts that we definitely have a different author at work here since this section is obviously much younger than the rest of the book.

A final nail in the coffin for verses 8b-20 is found in analyzing the grammar used here in relationship with the rest of the Gospel. When this is done, it is almost impossible to believe that these verses were written by the same person who wrote the rest of Mark. The sentence structure and overall style of these eleven verses vary significantly from what comes before them. Like a modern writer attempting to mimic Shakespeare, the differences are obvious and thus easily recognizable to the trained eye.

The Empty Tomb

Verses 1-8a themselves may give us one of our best clues as to why the early church felt uncomfortable with the original ending and why someone felt a need to tell the rest of the story. The eight verses that offer Mark's ending to Jesus' story center around the fact that when the women went to care for Jesus' body early on that first Easter morning, they discovered that the tomb was empty. This and the angel's words that Jesus was no longer there provide Mark's only evidence that Christ was alive. When you compare this with the other three Gospels, however, what you discover is that in Matthew, Luke, and John, the resurrection appearances themselves stood as the real proof that Jesus was alive.

This may be due to the fact that there are two major difficulties with the empty tomb account. First are the multiple legitimate competing theories as to why no body was at the tomb. Perhaps the women went to the wrong tomb. Or maybe someone had stolen the body. These ideas are perfectly rational and offer quick alternatives to the more difficult belief that Jesus overcame even death itself.

Beyond the alternate theories, what may have been even more problematic was the fact that all the Gospels write that the first witnesses to the empty tomb were women. In the biblical world, women could not testify in a court of law because their testimony was not regarded as trustworthy. This concern that the witness of the women at the tomb would have been dismissed may have been too much for early believers to overcome. This may in turn have led the other Gospel writers to center their writings on the resurrection appearances of the post-Easter Jesus rather than the empty tomb. Without accounts of these appearances, Mark as the first Gospel left the story open to much scrutiny and endless debate (Black, 104).

Too Open Ended . . .

Struggles with Mark's conclusion may have also centered on its open-ended nature. If one stops with verse 8a as do the oldest two Mark manuscripts, the Gospel finishes with these words: "So, they went out and fled from the tomb, for terror and amazement had seized them; and they said nothing to anyone, for they were afraid." How is one to understand such a concluding statement? This is a centuries-old struggle and is certainly a difficult ending for believers today, who prefer a more concrete statement regarding the resurrected Christ.

In his book *When Jesus Came to Harvard*, Harvey Cox points out that Jesus' style of teaching was in keeping with the best of Jewish rabbi tradition and had some significant characteristics. One aspect was that Jesus did not feel it was important to wrap things up neatly. Rather, Jesus preferred for his teaching to send the hearer away to think further about what had been said. Cox suggests that Jesus taught in a way that allowed for his words to be understood by different people on different levels at different times. Mark's ending seems to be in keeping with this idea. It forces the reader to think about what the ending means. What does it mean to leave the tomb both amazed and afraid? What is our own Galilee that the tomb calls us to travel to in order to meet the risen Savior? Does the tomb create in our mind doubt or faith (Cox, 27–28)?

It is easy to see why such an ending would be meaningful to some but troubling to others. One can understand why some in Mark's day may have been eager to preserve this type of ending but others quick to dismiss it and add a conclusion that was more palatable and less taxing on the mind.

Modern believers are like their Christian forefathers and fore-mothers at this point. In our postmodern world, we are more comfortable with answers than we are with open-ended questions. Our tendency is to grab hold of certainty while fleeing from anything that calls us to pursue our own meaning.

Other Features of Mark 16

This passage contains at least three other features that can be lost in our pursuit of an overall meaning. First, verse 1 reminds us that "Mary Magdalene, Mary the mother of James and Salome" were the first to encounter the empty tomb. While the four Gospels disagree as to the number and names of the women who were the first to arrive, they all agree that it was women who first encountered the empty tomb. This fact, in and of itself, is a significant truth to recognize. Evidently these women exhibited the most faithfulness and courage. While most of the disciples cowered behind closed doors, the women exhibited their devotion. Likewise, while not clearly spelled out in Mark, the other Gospels do record that these same women went and told the disciples what had happened. At its purest level, this means that these women were the first figures in the world to speak the good news that Christ was alive. This biblical reality certainly calls into question the belief that only men are meant to preach. After all, the first preachers seem to have been these women.

Another curious element of the text is the figure that the women encounter in verse 5. The text says it was a young man "dressed in a white robe, sitting at the right side" of the tomb. This individual tells the women that Jesus is alive again. Much debate has been focused on exactly who this person was. While no one knows for certain, the most likely possibility seems to be that this figure was an angel. Further, the idea that this was Jesus seems far-fetched. There is nothing in the text itself that connects the two. This idea does not seem to have received much support in serious scholarship, either.

Finally, the women are told in verse 7 to tell the disciples and Peter the good news that Jesus is alive and that he will meet them in Galilee. What is significant here is that the disciples are still loved and embraced by Christ, especially Peter, who is named separately from the larger group. After all, Peter had most emphatically denied his relationship with Christ through his remarks in the courtyard of the high priest in chapter 14. To say the least, these must have been welcome words to the eleven men who had so abandoned their Lord.

Life Lessons

In keeping with the proceeding comments, one must say that Mark 16 is a passage focused on inclusion, not exclusion. This truth may be quickly overlooked unless one closely considers the characters at the heart of the story. That women were the first at the tomb and the disciples were still embraced are rather amazing revelations. The key roles the women and the disciples play here offers a resounding note that the risen Christ is for all people. How in heaven's name can the church of today be so exclusionary when the first account of good news was so radically embracing?

The most important question here, though, has to revolve around how one is to understand and thus interact with this passage. In our session with the parable of the Sower, I made the point that it is important sometimes to leave things unsaid and the exact interpretation of an event unresolved. But the ending of Mark may take this reality even a step further with the way it ends the life of Jesus. Certainly no one can know how the author of Mark truly meant to end this Gospel. But we have to admit that the idea that Mark meant it to end just as it did with verse 8a is intriguing.

As with the ancient church, however, such a notion does not necessarily sit well with many in the modern church. Unfortunately, many modern believers want to be taught the gospel story and told exactly what any given text means. Rather than think for ourselves or allow our minds to wrestle with and reflect upon Scripture, we often want someone to wrap up things for us. This laziness prevents biblical texts from speaking to us and can thwart our ability to hear different meanings at different life stages.

I am not suggesting that explanations and possible lessons are not valuable to share, for such a methodology is followed in this session. Sometimes, though, our job is not to explain everything away, but rather to invite the hearer into a continual conversation with age-old texts.

In the end, which is better? Do we wish for someone to explain what it meant for the angel to say that the risen Jesus would meet his followers in Galilee? Or do we leave things as they are and trust that we will step into the text and wrestle with the meaning ourselves? I would argue for the latter: we *must* struggle with what Galilee means to us. Where is our Galilee? What does Jesus want to say to us there? And how will Jesus appear when we meet him? These are important questions. Unfortunately, when every aspect of the text is spelled out for us, we aren't challenged to wrestle with these questions.

1. How comfortable are you with how Mark ends in verse 8a? What is your biggest question about this abrupt conclusion?

_____

_____

_____

_____

_____

_____

2. Do you prefer the older ending of Mark, or are you more inclined to side with the alternate ending? What in particular leads you to your conclusion?

_____

_____

_____

_____

_____

_____

3. Does it trouble you that someone in the early church may have added to Mark? How do you feel about similar suggestions that are made in relation to other New Testament texts?

_____

_____

_____

_____

_____

_____

4. Are you most at ease when a passage is explained to you and little ambiguity remains, or are you more at home with an open-ended approach that allows some latitude in interpretation? Explain your answer.

_____

_____

_____

_____

_____

_____

5. When you study a biblical narrative, do you enter the story and allow yourself to become one of the characters, or do you maintain an outsider's viewpoint? What leads you to this way of interacting with the text?

_____

_____

_____

_____

_____

_____

6. Which surprises you more, the women as the first witnesses of the empty tomb or the fact that such resurrection grace is shown to the disciples despite their lack of faith during the crucifixion?

_____

_____

_____

_____

_____

_____

7. What does it mean to you to hear the angel say that the risen Lord can be met in Galilee? Where are the modern Galilees that we should be watching for the Lord?

_____

_____

_____

_____

_____

_____

Bibliography

Barclay, William. *The Gospel of Mark.* Louisville KY: John Knox Press, 2001.

————. *The Mind of Jesus.* SanFrancisco: HarperSanFrancisco, 1976.

Barton, Bruce B., et al. *Life Application Bible Commentary: Mark.* Wheaton IL: Tyndale House, 1994.

Black, Clifton. *Mark: Journey Through the Bible*, vol. 10. Nashville: Cokesbury, 1994.

Bock, Darrell L. *The Gospel of Mark: Cornerstone Commentary.* Wheaton IL: Tyndale Books, 2005.

Bodmer, Judy. *When Love Dies.* Nashville: Word Books, 1999.

Brown, Raymond. *Mark: The Savior for Sinners.* Nashville: Convention Press, 1978.

Carter, William. "After the Water Has Dried." Preached on Day One/ *The Protestant Hour.* 10 January 1999. Available online: http://www.day1.net/index.php5?view=transcripts&tid=300.

Chance, J. Bradley. "John the Baptist." In *Mercer Dictionary of the Bible.* Edited by Watson E. Mills et al. Macon GA: Mercer University Press, 1990.

Cole, R. Alan. *Mark: Tyndale New Testament Commentaries.* Grand Rapids MI: W. B. Eerdmans, 1989.

Conyers, A. J. *A Basic Christian Theology.* Nashville: Broadman and Holman, 1995.

Cox, Harvey. *When Jesus Came to Harvard: Making Moral Choices Today.* Boston: Houghton Mifflin Company, 2004.

Craddock, Fred B. *Luke.* Interpretation: A Biblical Commentary for Teaching and Preaching. Edited by James Luther Mays. Louisville: John Knox, 1990.

Culpepper, R. Alan. *Mark: Smyth & Helwys Bible Commentary.* Macon GA: Smyth & Helwys Publishers, 2007.

Dodd, C. H. *The Parables of the Kingdom.* London: Fontana, 1961.

Dowd, Sharyn. *Reading Mark: A Literary and Theological Commentary of the Second Gospel.* Macon GA: Smyth & Helwys, 2000.

Duckat, Walter. *Beggar to King: All the Occupations of Biblical Times.* Garden City NY: Doubleday, 1968.

Edwards, James. *The Gospel of Mark.* Cambridge UK: W. B. Eerdmans, 2002.

Evans, H. Walker, and Larry Richards. *The Book of Mark.* The Smart Guide to the Bible Series. Nashville: Nelson Books, 2007.

Garland, David. *The NIV Application Commentary on Mark.* Grand Rapids MI: Zondervan, 1996.

Green, Michael. *Who Is this Jesus?* Nashville: Thomas Nelson Publishers, 1990.

Hample, Stuart, and Eric Marshall, compilers. *Children's Letters to God.* New York: Workman, 1991.

Hickam, Homer. *The Coalwood Way.* New York: Delacorte Press, 2000.

Hunter, Archibald. *The Work and Words of Jesus.* Philadelphia: Westminster Press, 1973.

Kendall, R. T. *Understanding Theology: The Means of Developing a Healthy Church in the Twenty-first Century.* Fearn, Ross-shire, Scotland: Christian Focus Publications, 1999.

Kholoki, Sondos. "Alarming divorce rates amongst Muslims!" *Southern California InFocus* 3/1 (February 2007): 1. Available online: http://www.infocusnews.net/PDFs/InFocusOnline-Feb07.pdf.

Killinger, John. *A Devotional Guide to the Gospels.* Waco TX: Word Books, 1984.

Kittel, Gerhard, and Gerhard Friedrich, editors. *Theological Dictionary of the New Testament*. Grand Rapids: William B. Eerdmans, 1964.

Lenski, R. C. H. *Interpretation of Mark's Gospel*. Minneapolis: Augsburg Press, 1964.

Lester, Andrew D. *Coping with Your Anger*. Philadelphia PA: Westminster Press, 1983.

Leston, Stephen, Mark Strauss, and Ian Fair. *Matthew and Mark: Good News for Everyone*. Volume 8 of Quicknotes Commentary. Uhrichsville OH: Barbour Publishing, 2008.

Lewis, C. S. *Miracles*. San Francisco: HarperCollins, 2001.

Long, Thomas G. *Preaching and the Literary Forms of the Bible*. Philadelphia: Fortress, 1989.

Lopatto, Elizabeth. "Marrying smarter, later leading to decline in US divorce rate." *Boston Globe,* 12 May 2007. Available online: http://www.boston.com/news/nation/articles/2007/05/12/ marrying_smarter_later_leading_to_decline_in_us_divorce_ rate/.

Mashburn, T. J. III, and A. O. Collins. "Scribes in the New Testament." In *Mercer Dictionary of the Bible*. Edited by Watson E. Mills et al. Macon GA: Mercer University Press, 1990.

McGowan, James. *The Gospel of Mark*. Chattanooga: AMG Publishers, 2006.

"Monthly Vital Statistics Report." National Center for Health Statistics 39/12, supp. 2 (21 May 1991): 1-20. Available online: http://www.cdc.gov/nchs/data/mvsr/supp/mv39_12s2.pdf.

Moorehead, Kate. *Organic God*. Boston: Cowley, 2007.

Oden, Thomas C. *The Word of Life*. Peabody MA: Prince Press, 1998.

Robertson, A. T. *Studies in Mark's Gospel*. Revised and edited by Heber F. Peacock. Nashville: Broadman, 1978.

Saluter, Arlene F., and Terry A. Lugaila. "Marital Status and Living Arrangements: March 1996." Current Population Reports: Population Characteristics. Census Bureau, U. S. Department of Commerce, Economics and Statistics Administration. Available online: http://www.census.gov/prod/3/98pubs/p20-496.pdf.

Stein, Robert H. *Jesus the Messiah*. Leicester UK: InterVarsity Press, 1996.

Stookey, Laurence Hull. *Baptism: Christ's Act in the Church*. Nashville: Abingdon, 1982.

Talbert, Charles H. *Reading Luke*. New York: Crossroad, 1982.

Trafton, Joseph L. "Essenes." In *Mercer Dictionary of the Bible*. Edited by Watson E. Mills et al. Macon GA: Mercer University Press, 1990.

U.S. Census Bureau. "Most people make only one trip down the aisle, but first marriages shorter, Census Bureau reports." News release, 19 September 2007. Available online: http://www.census.gov/Press-Release/www/releases/archives/marital_status_living_arrangements/010624.html.

Williamson, Lamar Jr. *Mark*. Interpretation: A Biblical Commentary for Teaching and Preaching. Edited by James Luther Mays. Atlanta: John Knox, 1983.

Willis, Garry. *What Jesus Meant*. London: Penguin Books, 2007.

Wright, Bradley. "Statistics about Christian Divorce Rates." Bradley Wright's Weblog. http://brewright.blogspot.com/2006/12/christian-divorce-rates.html (19 December 2006).

Yaconelli, Mike. *Messy Spirituality*. Grand Rapids MI: Zondervan, 2002.